RAILROADS

OF THE

CIVIL WAR

RAILROADS

OF THE

CIVIL WAR

AN ILLUSTRATED HISTORY

MICHAEL LEAVY

WESTHOLME
Yardley

Acknowledgments

This work would never have gotten "on track" were it not for the abundant research material and photographs made available by the Library of Congress and the National Archives. The author is grateful to both for making their resources so easily accessible to the public.

Frontispiece: A train bringing a load of supplies for the Union Army up from the wharf at City Point, Virginia (detail); see page 35. (*Library of Congress*)

First Westholme Paperback 2019

Copyright ©2010 Michael Leavy

Westholme Publishing, LLC
904 Edgewood Road
Yardley, Pennsylvania 19067
Visit our Web site at www.westholmepublishing.com

ISBN: 978-1-59416-329-6

Printed in the United States of America.

for Rebecca

Contents

Veterans and their families gather for the dedication of the monument on the Bull Run battlefield, June 11, 1865. (*Library of Congress*)

INTRODUCTION

Nearly a century and a half have passed since the last guns fell silent in the American Civil War, yet it lingers in our collective subconscious. Scholars continue to review and rework the data into increasingly complex theories about what led to this national catastrophe, but for the folks back then who suffered through it, the reasons were plain enough. The war was fought over slavery. Other causes descend from that singular issue in varying degrees of importance.

From 1861 through 1865 a river of blood flowed through this country. An estimated six hundred twenty thousand out of a population of about thirty-one million died as a result of the war. Some theorize that actual civilian losses may have pushed it closer to seven hundred thousand deaths.

Staggering numbers of casualties rise like apparitions from battlefields with names such as Gettysburg, the Wilderness, and Antietam. As is often the case, wars of this enormity consume all who are in it. The war comes to control men instead of the other way around. Otherwise gentle, peace-loving and hard-working men are transformed into savage killers. A rush of technology, inspired by a kind of madness, leads to larger and more deadly weapons and greater casualties.

Within the hell wind of fire and screams comes an uneasy notion that humanity has either regressed or that this sacrifice will lead to better human understanding.

It might be reasonable to think that life was cheap back then. Or that faith in America allowed that generation to tolerate such losses. It may be beyond our ability to comprehend the incredible suffering they endured. The images of destroyed cities and towns seem impossible. Yet the seas of rubble that were Richmond, Fredericksburg, and Atlanta tell us that if we can do this to ourselves and survive—we can survive just about anything.

Perhaps that is the richest lesson of the Civil War: the Republic was indeed worth saving. The nation obviously has a willingness to forgive that relieves tensions and allows us to absorb and bounce back from a Civil War, world wars, and terrorist attacks. Sometimes we come back stronger than before.

Had the South won, the United States may have developed as two mediocre nations; possibly three if the developing West saw the fractured nation as a failed experiment and chose to go its own way. The latter may have been in Lincoln's thoughts as he quickly set about tying California and the West to the rest of the nation by means of the First Transcontinental Railroad. The South saw things differently. The massive endeavor felt more like a noose slowly closing around its neck. Northern Republican's obsession to keep slavery from spreading to the western states sometimes usurped their desire to keep the South as part of the Union. Yet, they anguished that if they lost control of the South, slavery might continue to spread throughout the Western Hemisphere. In the end, however, the symbolic power of the country united by a railroad would be encouraging to a mourning and heart-broken population.

Studies of the strategies of the Civil War cannot lose sight of the price paid in blood. In contemporary analysis of the costs of the war, those killed are listed in charts as "Loss of Human Capital," essentially an economic statistic. Without being maudlin, this book looks at the impact of railroads in the war while not ignoring the human price. No other war has caused so much emotional and financial stress to this nation. The cost of emancipation was devastating and would have wrecked a lesser nation.

A naive and unsuspecting population expected that hostilities would not last long—months perhaps. But both sides dug in and early Southern victories suggesting they wanted to bring the war north, which led to abrupt escalations.

Railroads were immediately employed on both sides, becoming critical to almost all strategies. The railroad not only allowed the war to range over great distances at high speeds but also led to its duration and subsequent carnage. The story of brave railroad men on both sides is often overlooked in studies of the war but their role was crucial and determinant. Theirs is a story of machines and muscle—of bravery and adventure.

In the spring of 1865 General Robert E. Lee would be forced to surrender his Army of Northern Virginia because trains bringing supplies into Appomattox Station were overtaken by Union cavalry. Ultimately the railroads that prolonged and enlarged the war would become the mechanism by which it would end.

RAILROADS

OF THE

CIVIL WAR

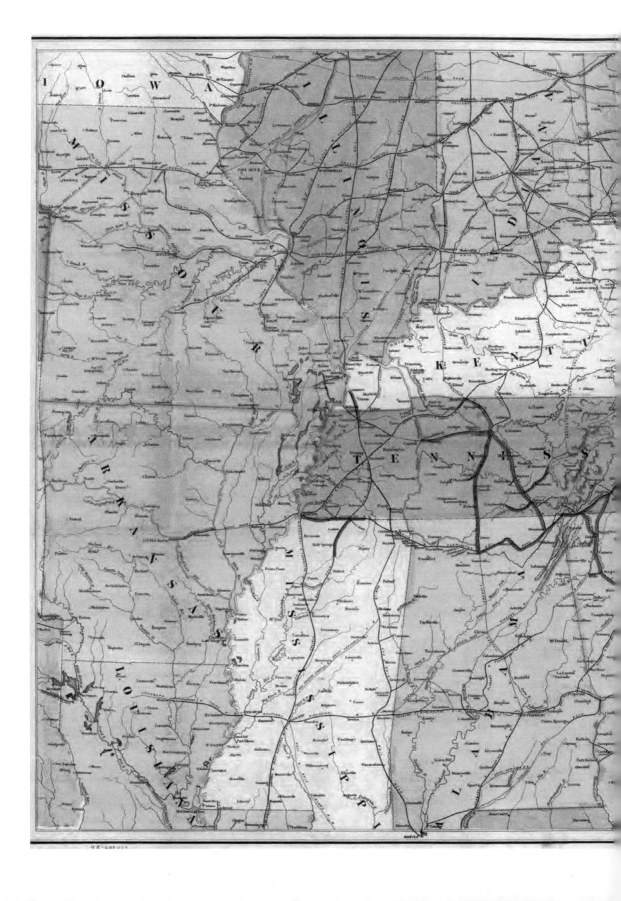

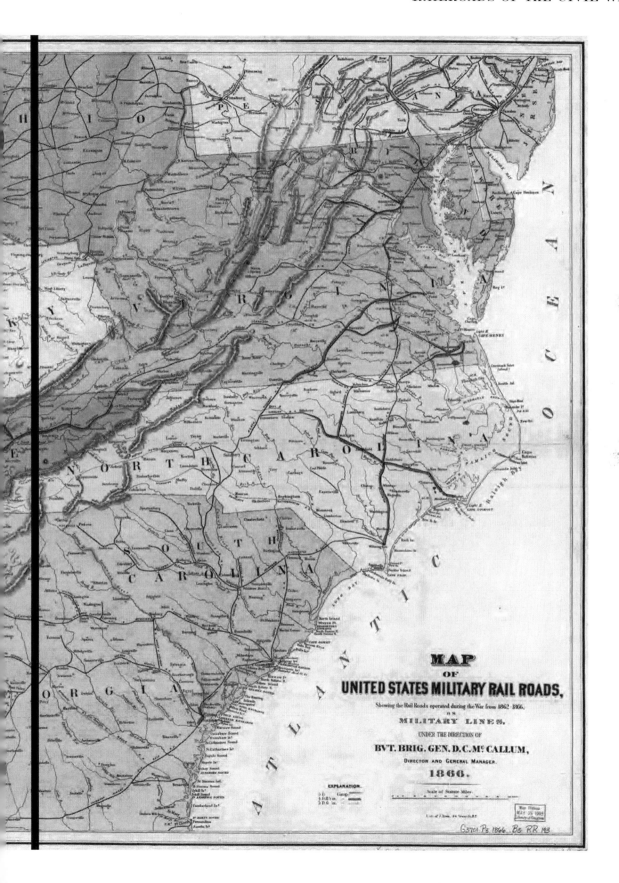

MAP
OF
UNITED STATES MILITARY RAIL ROADS,

Showing the Rail Roads operated during the War from 1862-1866,
ON
MILITARY LINES.

UNDER THE DIRECTION OF

BVT. BRIG. GEN. D.C. McCALLUM,

DIRECTOR AND GENERAL MANAGER.

1866.

The first direct military use of the railroad occurred during the Crimean War. A track was laid across Crimea from the harbor at Balaklava to Sevastapool in order to expedite ammunition and supplies to British and French troops. Here the railway bed is being prepared. Iron rails and other supplies can been seen in this photo taken in 1855 by Roger Fenton. (*Library of Congress*)

ONE

THIS NEW APPLIANCE OF WAR

"There is a terrible war coming, and these young men who have never seen war cannot wait for it to happen, but I tell you, I wish that I owned every slave in the South, for I would free them all to avoid this war."
—*Robert E. Lee*

Railroads became a mania that swept America and Europe starting in the 1830s. Trains could move people and freight much faster. Aside from pockets of poverty, America was a unique nation from the start. In spite of the evil institution of slavery, immigrants came here in droves seeking personal liberty and the opportunities freedom offered. And from the start America was an impatient country. Technologies advanced often at phenomenal rates. This was no less the case with railroads. They were noisy, mysterious, dangerous, and mesmerizing. Ultimately they would navigate America through its phenomenal industrial growth leading it to worldwide preeminence.

Regardless of where the early trains ran, on the whole they were a maintenance nightmare, moody, dangerous, prone to breakdowns and stalling, while being endlessly demanding of fuel. But compared to their biological counterparts (horses, mules, and oxen) they were a phenomenon, capable of transporting more tonnage at a speed and rate of at least ten to one. Animals needed to rest, were frequently stubborn, and became easily hobbled.

Mechanized transportation was not new in America. The first adaptations of steam engines to propel vehicles in America happened in 1787 when John Fitch powered a boat on the Delaware River. This was followed by James Rumsey doing the same thing on the Potomac. These events stirred the first inklings of the coming transportation revolution. Some crude horse drawn railroads where cars were drawn along wood rails began to appear in the early 1800s. Later improvements to rail would include attaching strap iron to the top of wood rails. Eventually solid iron rail would be used. It was first attached to flat stones and later to wooden ties.

Steam propulsion of ships was well underway when John Stevens demonstrated a steam-powered machine on tracks in 1826. The first railroad charters in North America were issued as early as 1815 but work didn't begin in earnest until the mid to late 1820s. Contrary to beliefs that train service began in

A German engraving from 1831 showing the steam train operating between Liverpool and Manchester, England. Once steam-powered locomotives proved practical, railways quickly sprang up across England and other countries, including the United States. (*Library of Congress*)

1831 on the Baltimore & Ohio, the first service was actually on the Charleston & Hamburg in South Carolina on Christmas Day 1830.

Improvements in the steam piston engine led to more power and efficiency. The double-acting steam engine directed high-pressure steam alternately on both faces of the piston. A slide valve allowed steam to enter and then exit the cylinder. This exerted power on the drive rods which in turn, rotated the drive wheels. The "choo-choo" sound associated with a steam locomotive is caused by the exhaust as it exits the cylinder.

The earliest railroads were not always met with universal love. They were noisy, dirty, dangerous, and quite political. They were in commercial competition with canals, which were often the source of regional pride and the glory of politicians who fought to route the waterways through their towns and cities. Railroad owners were wily though in convincing politicians the rail lines would enhance the canals. They even subjugated their interests to the canals, somehow knowing the great advantages of steam would usurp canal transportation sooner rather than later. Among the fledgling railroads to compete with canals were those in the vicinity of New York's Erie Canal. Perhaps the most inarguable advantage Northern railroads had was that they could operate during winter when canals were either frozen over or drained.

Gradually railroad companies were able to bend public sentiment their way. Many of the first railroads provided passenger service, paralleling the canals or careening across the landscape from one population center to the next. At a time when state and federal regulations on commerce were not nearly as intrusive as they are now, the railroads wandered seemingly willy-nilly with no overriding purpose other than to provide stockholders with profits. It wasn't until the 1840s that the feasibility of transporting produce and commodities at low cost over long distances was demonstrated. A combination of land grants, subsidies, and private investments led to a railroad building surge in the 1850s.

Soon railroads were taking over the canals which they had previously deferred to. It was not unusual for a rail company to lay track along the canal's towpath—the drained canal prism beside them being abandoned to weeds and debris. The Irish, German, and Chinese immigrants who had dug the canals and built the stone locks were now employed by rail companies to lay tracks, build structures and bridges, and work the jobs required to maintain the system. In the South, slaves—many leased from planters to build southern canals—were now used to build regional lines.

The revolution in transportation can be demonstrated with the James River and Kanawha Canal through the western counties of Virginia. The canal was surveyed by George Washington. Work began in 1785, and after several financial failures, was only half completed by 1851. Railroads were already proving more proficient in transporting passengers and commodities to the coast. After the Civil War, the State of Virginia—which had financed the canal, had not the funds to support the old water artery. The slaves who built it—slaves who had been made to slog through mud up to their knees, were now free. In 1873 the canal company built a small rail line to connect the waterway with the Chesapeake & Ohio Railway. In 1878 both the canal and railroad were sold to the Richmond & Allegheny Railroad. The towpath where African Americans, known as Bateaumen, once guided mules pulling flat-bottomed boats now supported a railroad track.

By the 1860s, trains were an integral part of American culture. They altered cities, generated new industries, and created thousands of jobs. Growing demands for transporting livestock, freight, and passengers further and faster led to larger locomotives, sturdier freight equipment, and more comfortable passenger cars.

Industrialization predominated in the North and increasingly in the West. This brought larger population centers requiring more food, merchandise, and improved transportation. Yankee industrial capitalists, disgusted by slavery but indifferent to their own abuses such as child labor, long hours, and sweat shops, did their parts to open fissures between the North and South. At the same time the export of Southern short-sta-

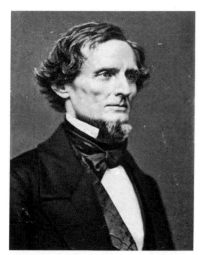

Jefferson Davis, Secretary of War under President Millard Fillmore and future President of the Confederate States of America, neglected to organize a formidable challenge to Lincoln's United States Military Railroads system during the Civil War. This had much to do with the South's defeat. Southern railroads cooperated to the fullest but they were compensated with worthless bonds. They would have great difficulty keeping their lines operational due mostly to lack of parts. (*Library of Congress*)

ple cotton accounted for nearly half of the country's exports. All parts of the country benefited from this and Northern industrialists profited from the economic opportunities it presented. The South produced two-thirds of the world's cotton. Slavery allowed cotton to be produced cheaper than anywhere else on earth.

Meanwhile, the California gold rush created waves of immigration to the far West. The North, eager to keep the West part of the nation, enticed them with talk of a railroad that would connect the Atlantic with the Pacific. In 1854, then Secretary of War Jefferson Davis, dispatched survey parties to survey preliminary routes. He of course favored a southern one. When his preference was rejected, the first seed of his anti-union stance was planted. Throughout the 1850s the South had been suspicious and envious of the favoritism lavished on Westward developers. Attempts to legislate a Homestead Act giving 160 acres to anyone wishing to settle in the West deepened Southerners' anxieties. The policy's unspoken intention was to attract free-soilers to the area in order to restrict slaveholders from establishing large plantations in those territories.

The problem of slavery had plagued the country from the beginning. It was America's curse, a system in place before the colonies rebelled against England to unite under a separate flag. Slavery and other forms of bondage had long existed in the New World. Indians held slaves—usually members of other tribes captured in battle. And there were the Dutch Patroonships; a feudal tenant system established during the Dutch colonial days. Vast land grants along the Hudson River saw rise to magnificent mansions. The "Lords of the Manor" oversaw their plantations where tenant farmers existed in hopeless poverty. Schools, homes, and churches were provided by the small plantation towns but there were also cruel overseers, tax collectors, and hangmen.

A lesser form of bondage was apprenticeship. Although not wholly a bad scheme, it lent itself to abuses. Young apprentices, usually boys, were often held in harsh servitude for years, being made to work long hours, confined to small rooms, and often beaten and abused in other ways. Newspapers of the day ran ads for rewards for the return of runaway apprentices.

Increasingly regional disputes over slavery began to bubble to the surface. Storm clouds gathered. In 1853, Harriet Beecher Stowe's antislavery novel, *Uncle Tom's Cabin*, incited much controversy. Anxieties continued to fester during the 1850s. The Underground Railroad steadily developed its network of routes along which slaves could escape to freedom in Canada to avoid Fugitive Slave Acts which ordered the return of slaves caught in the North. Abolitionists and organized national societies and conventions became bolder in their antislavery oratory.

Lincoln and his "Radical Republicans," as they were called then, were bent on preventing the spread of slavery not only in the new territories but elsewhere in the hemisphere. The 1860 U.S. census recorded a population of 31,183,582 of which 3,950,528 were slaves, the latter comprising 13 percent of the entire population. The total number of slaveholders was 393,975. Modern re-evaluations intent on deflecting the primary causes away from slavery fall short when played against President Jefferson Davis's own words spoken on April 29, 1861, in Montgomery, Alabama, during ratification of the Constitution of the Confederate States of America. He brings a disturbing logic to the issue of slavery and how it was protected in the U.S. Constitution. He further explains how the industrialized North rejected slavery while the South, remaining agricultural, needed slaves. Increasingly the North condemned the slave-holding states, which provoked regional fracturing.

In his address, Davis points out the North's hypocrisy:

The climate and soil of Northern States soon proved unpropitious to the continuance of slave labor, whilst the converse was the case at the South. Under the unrestricted free intercourse between the two sections, the Northern States consulted their own interests by selling their slaves to the South and prohibiting slavery within their limits. The South were willing purchasers of a property suitable to their wants, and paid the price of the acquisition without harboring a suspicion that their quiet possession was to be disturbed by those who were inhibited not only by want of constitutional authority, but by good faith as vendors, from disquieting a title emanating from themselves. As soon, however, as the Northern States that prohibited Africa slavery within their limits had reached a number sufficient to give their representation a controlling voice in the Congress, a persistent and organized system of hostile measures against the rights of the owners of slaves in the Southern States was inaugurated and gradually extended.

This brief analysis of the issues leading to the war is important because it shows how the nation grew apart—an industrialized North and agricultural South—with enormous moral and cultural differences. The fact that most of the war was fought on Southern soil should have given the South strategic advantages. Its resources were at hand to fend off the Northern onslaught, but since its industrial infrastructure was restricted—particularly through the lack of extensive railroads—it would not be able to effectively increase its manufacturing output—firearms, locomotives, ammunition, and other military goods—to help repulse the Northern advances.

Manufactured in England in 1828, the *Stourbridge Lion* was the first locomotive to operate in the United States when it ran on a test track in Honsdale, Pennsylvania, in August 1829. (*Library of Congress*)

Before the American Civil War, England was the leader in locomotive development and construction, and provided the American market with superior products. As more railroads were chartered, the demand for native-built machines gave rise to many domestic locomotive works. England would continue to benefit, however, with sales of wheels, rails, and other railroad-related products to America. If nothing else, their steel wheels were vastly superior to those made in America at the time.

Some railroads, such as the Baltimore & Ohio, were capable of building their own machines. Most of the major builders were in the Mid-Atlantic States. One of the more prolific builders was Rogers Locomotive Works in Paterson, New Jersey. Also known as Rogers, Ketchum and Grosvenor, it would produce about 900 machines between 1835 and 1867. Norris Locomotive Works and Baldwin Locomotive Works, both in Philadelphia, would produce a combined 2,000 machines between the late 1830s and the start of the war. Mason Machine Works in Taunton, Massachusetts, in addition to textile machinery, built 100 locomotives.

Southern production of machines was much less by comparison. Talbott and Brother Iron Works in Richmond rolled a few engines from its shops. Appomattox Locomotive Works in Petersburg, Virginia, produced fewer than two dozen machines. The largest manufacturer was Tredegar Iron Works, producing about 70 machines in the 1850s. Often railroads produced their own passenger cars and other rolling stock such as box, flat, and stock cars.

A standard 4-4-0 locomotive and tender built between 1850-1865 could cost $6,000 to $19,000. Price was determined primarily by weight, with the average machine weighing between 24 and 36 tons. The tenders were usually 20 tons. Depending on luxury— or lack thereof—a passenger coach cost around $2,200. As passenger service developed, railroads competed by offering cushioned seats, attractive wood carving, brass attachments, sleeping quarters, and stoves for long winter journeys.

William Mason of Mason Machine Works was a master builder of locomotives and something of an industrial artist. His machines were handsome with balanced lines and tended to be not overly adorned. Thomas Rogers and his Rogers Locomotive and Machine Works—founded in 1832—was very quality-minded as well. Rogers himself inspected every inch of iron that went into his boilers. He preferred Yorkshire plate from England over American or Sligo charcoal iron.

Boiler barrels were formed with telescoping rings, each sliding together with lap joints that were riveted. The first locomotive boilers were sheathed or lagged in wood for insulation. By the time of the Civil War many boilers were covered with sheet-iron placed over layers of felt. Russian iron was favored especially for prominent passenger engines. The Russians had developed a technique of hammering graphites into iron to slow deterioration and rusting. The surface was then polished to a mirror-like finish.

Depending on the graphites used and the degree of polishing, the boiler took on beautiful shimmering colorations ranging from blue to gray to greens. The boiler seams were covered with brass bands. Workers would sometimes polish the locomotive with sperm whale oil, bringing it to a high luster.

Other parts of the locomotive and tender were richly detailed with Victorian flourishes that included ornate bell holders and headlamp supports. Copper and brass attachments together with rich wood cabs, glass gauges and flags were other appealing adornments. It was not unusual to paint trimmings with various reds, greens, blues and yellows. The tenders and headlamps could have hand-painted frescoes or portraits. In all, a locomotive was a moving work of art. The existing hand-colored lithographs from the time confirm this.

Standard locomotive plans could be modified to accommodate regional considerations such as track gauges, fuel supplies, and grades. The 4-4-0 wheel arrangement, introduced in 1837, was by far the most popular. By the time of the Civil War the "American" type 4-4-0 was the prevailing engine in use across the nation. At the front of this type of locomotive was a four-wheeled pilot truck for distributing weight and tracking around curves and through switches. In the center were four main drive wheels (drivers). There were no trailer trucks or drivers towards the back of the machine.

Cars and locomotives were coupled with a link and pin arrangement that were perpetually troublesome. Coupler assemblies often varied from railroad to railroad. This made connecting cars from different lines difficult and time consuming. Sometimes numerous pins had to be tried before a properly fitting one was found. The yardman connecting the cars had a harrowing job as he directed the engineer. All too often the yardman was injured—losing fingers or an arm. Many were killed.

Mainline engines included a headlamp, a bell for letting people know the train was nearing a crossing or station, and a shrill whistle to project signals. Yard engines traditionally didn't have headlamps as a matter of expense since the tendency was to make up trains (couple cars together) during daylight.

With multiple trains traveling back and forth along a single mainline, signaling was a critical science. With increased wartime traffic, dispatching and signaling was certainly vexing. There were numerous accidents with soldiers being killed or maimed. Sadly some of this was the result of drunkenness. Young soldiers expecting the war to be a source of adventure and delights had darker thoughts when packed into boxcars and sent jostling at high speeds down uncertain tracks with the very real chance of derailment.

The development of the military telegraph service would improve matters. Poles were placed alongside the tracks allowing communication among stations, field camps, ports, and key cities. Over 15,000 miles of telegraph line dedicated to military use by the North would be built during the Civil War and maintained by a civilian bureau overseen by the Quartermaster's Department.

The established system of train operation involved running them on a timetable. Schedules were drawn up in advance with every crew knowing the time their train could operate within a section—or block—of track. Prior to the telegraph, there could be no rescheduling; woe to any engineer coming unexpectedly upon a wreck or train off schedule! By the time he saw it, it was usually too late. Obviously, trains cannot swerve to avoid collision and they need time and space to decelerate.

The telegraph reduced much of this. Messages could be sent ahead, faster than the train, allowing for a suitable change in timetable schedules through train orders. All those involved in train movements had to focus on timing. Clocks and pocket watches had to be synchronized. A mistake involving even a few seconds could lead to disaster.

The block system allows one train in a section of track at a time to avoid collisions. The blocks, anywhere from one to six miles long, also permitted trains headed in the opposite direction to enter the mainline from sidings and runaround tracks. During the 1830s, all this was coordinated by signalmen located along the mainline. Using hand signals and lanterns, they kept trains on schedule, warned of delays, and responded to engineers signaling up the line with locomotive bells and whistles. During the 1850s and 1860s, fixed mechanical signals, controlled by levers worked by the signalman, came into use.

Track gauges presented problems. There were at least ten different gauges in the North alone before the Civil War, including the Erie Railroad's sprawling six-foot gauge. Railroad owners were initially opposed to standardizing track gauges because they thought having their own track gauge gave them an advantage over competitors. Lucrative fees were charged for transferring freight from one line to another. State legislators stubbornly opposed standardization as well. But the folly of different gauges became immediately evident. As transportation of commodities expanded, it was difficult for one railroad to transfer its cars to another if the gauges did not match. Some railroads tried dual gauges to accommodate connecting lines but it too proved unsatisfactory.

In 1853, ten small railroads in upstate New York were amalgamated into the New York Central. Individually the lines were insignificant, providing basic regional needs. Connected, they became part of a powerful network. Track gauges and equipment were gradually standardized and the independent lines were realigned to allow uninterrupted travel from Albany to Buffalo. It was sign of things to come.

The idea of a standard gauge of four-feet-eight-and-one-half inches gradually took hold in the North and became the more sensible course. Companies could now send freight to connecting lines without the delay of transferring cargoes. This cooperation between railroads was offset through payment of transfer fees and in some cases trackage rights.

Southern railroads actually had foresight, with a five-foot gauge predominating in the Deep South before the war. Gaps between railroads in towns and cities, however, would compromise this advantage. Local officials wanted passengers to spend the night in hotels while teamsters profited from unloading freight from one railroad and then reloading it on a line across town. Another reason for keeping railroads out of a town's center was the real possibility of a locomotive starting a fire. Embers from a locomotive's stack could easily alight on a wooden station, burning it down and other nearby buildings. It was safer to keep trains outside the town limits. Also, despite the popularity of a five-foot gauge in the South, the multitude of gauges along the Border States would cause problems in transportation in the coming war.

⚜

The American Civil War has been called the first "modern war." A number of technologies converged and accelerated along with the railroad during the conflict. Among them were the repeating rifle, the submarine, observation balloons, photography, and electricity—primarily through the use of the telegraph system. The electric telegraph was the most important source of communications during the conflict. (President Lincoln, for example, would sleep at the telegraph office waiting for news on battles.)

If the notion of this being the first modern war is accepted, railroads had a lot to do with it. They were a principal factor in nearly every strategy to the point where the use and control of railroads became the strategy. In addition, the railroad's capacity to expand the scope of the war contributed to an increase in human suffering and destruction of population centers. The interior and exterior line strategies of Napoleonic warfare were instantly outdated. The use of railroads changed the dynamics of how soldiers could be moved to confront enemy armies. As railroads became the lifeline—or death line—of the war, battles tended to develop near railheads. Replacements could be brought in faster, prolonging battles and increasing casualties.

Large armies trudging lengthy distances down crude rural roads with wagons, horses, and mules—as was the case with the War for Independence—became less common; it became a tactic reserved for smaller raiding parties or soldiers moving down gaps between railroads.*

Tradition fixes the official commencement of the Civil War with actions in Charleston Harbor when shots were exchanged between Fort Sumter and Confederate batteries around the harbor. An important action prior to this and another catalyst for the war was John Brown's raid on the arsenal and gun manufactory at Harper's Ferry on October

---

*An exception to this during the Civil War was Sherman's daring and personal lunge into the heart of the Confederacy. With limited supply lines on his march from Atlanta to Savannah, he insisted on isolation, even cutting off telegraph communication at times. To accumulate supplies and food for his men after having severed his railroad supply line, he employed a strategy of foraging, sending groups of "Bummers" to raid farms and towns. The foraging was also part of a strategy of terror that included laying waste to population centers. Chief among his objectives was wrecking railroads. He reasoned the Confederacy could produce all the ammunition it wanted but it was worthless without a means of transporting it.

18, 1859. The picturesque town in a ravine where the Potomac and Shenandoah Rivers form a juncture dated to 1761 when Robert Harper began a ferry service across the Potomac. Both Thomas Jefferson and George Washington had special affections for the place. In 1799 Washington established the United States Armory and Arsenal at Harper's Ferry and some of his family members moved to the community. His great-great nephew, Colonel Lewis Washington, would be held hostage during Brown's assault. In 1834 the Baltimore & Ohio Railroad began through service and established a railhead at what was already a thriving industrial colony.

John Brown, a determined abolitionist, led 17 men (five of them black) in the raid on the arsenal. Brown intended to capture weapons to supply a slave uprising in the South. Local authorities quickly suppressed the raiders and on October 18, a train brought 18 marines to the site. Under the command of Colonel Robert E. Lee, the raiders were quickly captured or killed. John Brown was later hanged. The failed raid, in which several railroad men were killed, stunned the nation.

Leaders in the North and South were not long in realizing the importance of railroads in military management. The first use of railroads to support a military conflict came in the 1840s during the war with Mexico where, because of their scarcity, they were used modestly to transport troops west. (The first railroad built specifically for warfare was the line built at Balaclava during the Crimean War in 1855.) When the Civil War broke out in 1861, railroads were an established part of the American way of life. During the pro-

longed war, Harper's Ferry would change hands seven times, much of it because of the importance of its rail facilities. Success in war depends on logistics; the ability to secure supplies and move them and soldiers efficiently. Armies in the past reached distant battlefronts by foot or with the use of animals. Their ability to sustain themselves progressively decreased the further they got from their supply bases. This often left armies raggedly destitute and starved, such as Napoleon's infamous retreat from Moscow. Railroads could now transport men, animals, and supplies up to ten times faster.

In January 1862, a War Department agency was established, the United States Military Rail Roads (USMRR). Federal legislation gave the military authority over railroads and the telegraph system. President Lincoln restricted use of this new power primarily to Southern railroads captured during the war. Under the direction of Brigadier General Herman Haupt, the USMRR was critical to the Union war effort. New train tracks were rapidly laid down into enemy territory. Haupt also utilized highly trained cavalry raiders to destroy Confederate railroads and disrupt operations.

The USMRR expanded its rail network by assimilating southern railroads as each was captured and then laying miles of new track to develop new hubs and bases. The North's commercial railroads were only too happy to cooperate with federal requests. The escalating conflict became a boon for them as much as it was for undertakers and coffin makers. There were incidents of shameless corruption and overcharging both by railroad officials and politicians but overall the system worked.

With astonishing quickness the efficient USMRR Construction Corps laid miles of tracks into otherwise sleepy port towns and cities. Virtually overnight heavily burdened schooners and steamboats arrived at newly-built wharves where they unloaded tons on supplies that included food, tools, clothes, weapons, tents, and other sundries. A rush of trains redistributed it to the front. Large transports brought in thousands of troops to be rushed by trains to distant battles. Any location with reach of a railroad could become a battleground. The sizes of armies quickly doubled and tripled.

By 1864, Major General William T. Sherman could rely on a single-track line between Atlanta and Louisville nearly 500 miles long to supply his 100,000 men on their rampage through the South. The Confederacy was unable to effectively mobilize its railroads because Northern advances had forced it, in many instances, to destroy its precious engines and rolling stock to keep them out of Yankee hands.

The South clung to the tenants of States Rights, having a very American aversion to federal intrusions—something they were currently trying to break away from. As a result, with little central governmental authority, incompetence and confusion at the highest levels prevented the South from developing a similar rail network to battle the North's USMRR—or to at least to put in place some system to protect their railroads from being devoured by the Union. This strategic blunder was a major factor in the South's defeat. Later in the war the Confederate government started exercising some authority over states, such as ordering plantation owners to release their slaves to

Personnel of the United States Military Rail Roads pose for a photograph in 1864. (*Library of Congress*)

help repair railroads, but by that time the war was essentially over.

Despite being proud of their railroads, the South's rail systems were ill prepared for a sustained war. Combined they had a running mileage of only 9,000 miles compared to 20,000 miles in the North. The main purpose of Southern railroads was to transport cotton and produce from inland plantations to port towns along rivers, especially the Mississippi, and along the seacoast. In addition to cotton, rice and lumber were important materials destined for European markets. New England clothing mills depended on steady deliveries of cotton as well. Still, with no great urbanization across the South, there was little need to develop more substantial rail networks.

Shortly after secession the South began its mobilization with deep regrets they had not stockpiled rail supplies beforehand, much of which came from the North or England. Southern commercial activity would come to a virtual halt. Railroads had to let many workers go. President Jefferson Davis appealed to railroad owners to aid the "Cause" by transporting men and supplies for the Confederacy at no charge. Of course this practice could not last. When owners did start charging rates, they were paid with government bonds that were practically worthless. Meanwhile the men they let go were now gone for good, many having entered the military. From the start Southern railroads were financially backed against a wall, being rendered incapable of sustaining themselves—this in spite of their lower operating costs resulting from slave labor.

With railroad supplies scarce the Confederate government encouraged railroad owners to send agents to Europe to purchase locomotive tires, car wheels, spikes, axles—virtually anything they could obtain to help keep their lines operational. Getting it back to America was another matter. Southern railroad owners would develop ways for getting these supplies through the Union's blockade of Southern ports but it would prove too little, too late.

In contrast, Northern railroads running towards Washington were being double-tracked. Thousands of troops and supplies were being moved daily without interruption to normal freight and passenger service. Additionally, canals and maritime activity thrived.

At the beginning of the war the South had about 1,500 locomotives. Many of these were out of service by 1864 because of lack of replacement parts. Iron tires could last up to 60,000 miles with normal usage. Highly valued steel tires lasted up to 200,000 miles. There was a dismal shortage of iron for rails

and few rolling mills to produce them. The secessionist states preferred rail from England. Apparently it was of higher quality than that obtained from Northern suppliers. Now they would settle for anything they could get.

The Confederate's largest rolling mill was Tredegar Iron Works near Richmond. Its location had as much to do with the Confederacy choosing Richmond for its capital as any other consideration. The mill would produce half of the 2,200 cannon used by the Confederacy. In business since 1843, its peacetime fabricating capacities were remarkable, producing rail, wheels, gauges, and locomotives. Shortly into the war however, pig-iron supplies became virtually exhausted, causing Tredegar to shut down for a month. Through resourcefulness and determination, the iron works would employee 2,500 by 1863, producing even bricks, shoes, ornamental ironwork, as well as 12-pound Napoleon bronze cannon and railroad equipment.

The scarcity of raw materials would continue to plague Tredegar, bringing work to a halt in March 1865—a month before the end of the war. A battalion of 350 employees had to protect the factory then from mobs during the evacuation of Richmond. The Union seized Tredegar and held it for four months after the war. It was returned to Southern ownership shortly thereafter and, with hefty investments from Virginia capitalists, would come to play an important role in Reconstruction.

During the war, Tredegar's owner, Joseph Anderson, was more sympathetic to the needs of railroads since he had produced engines and was grateful for their bringing him his raw materials. They also transported his finished products, be it ornamental wrought iron for New Orleans's buildings or re-bored cannon for the military. More personally, they brought meat from stockyards for his employees.

Prior to the war, the South's railroads met their needs but many were in questionable condition. For the most part they ran on worn light or "U" rail that needed re-rolling or splicing. There was little ballasted track. Many bridges were so rickety engineers said a prayer as they eased their locomotives on to them. Some bridges in the Deep South were said to sink four to five inches into swampy creek beds from the weight of trains only to spring back up once a train had crossed.

Another matter that caused anxiety among Southern railroad owners was the Confederate Navy's sudden fascination with ironclads. In some cases lesser railroads were disrupted when their good rail was seized by the CSN and replaced—if at all—with nearly worthless rail. Some of the better "acquired" rail was sent to more important roads but it was more likely to be melted and re-forged as ironclad plating. An average ship required roughly 500 tons of iron. The Confederacy needed nearly 12,000 tons for plating its planned armada. This did not include what was needed for armaments. The combined tonnage may have produced roughly 200 miles of track depending on the weight of the rail. This may seem insignificant but considering the savviness of some Southern generals, a few good miles of track laid in the right place at the right time may have changed the outcome of some important battles.

The Confederacy conducted many bold railroad operations, most notably raids that interrupted enemy advances through wholesale destruction of track and equipment. Elite partisan raiders fearlessly and savagely attacked this coal-burning dragon—the USMRR—sent to help subjugate them. Using passion and cunning they often delivered crippling blows to better-provisioned and sometimes over-burdened Northern forces. Stonewall Jackson's operations against the Baltimore & Ohio shut much of that railroad down for almost a year. A carefully placed horseshoe on a rail would send a train spilling down an embankment. Innovation is the best friend of the underdog.

The South's mindset, overall, may have longed for the golden days of Old Dixieland but it was hardly old fashioned in how it dealt with the blue clad invader. Robert E. Lee was among the first to contemplate a rail-borne cannon. The Confederate navy came up with the first ironclad. They further challenged the North with submarines, torpedo boats, underwater mines, and rams. The war ended with Grant and Lee at Appomattox but the final Confederate surrender was actually November 6, 1865 aboard the commerce raider CSS *Shenandoah* in Liverpool, England.

Ironically, the Confederacy is credited with construction of the first military railroad in America. The Centreville Military Railroad was a 5.5-mile spur off the Orange & Alexandria Railroad. Built by the Confederate States Army between November 1861 and February 1862, it ran east of Manassas Junction in Virginia to a point along the south side of the Centreville Plateau, passing Bull Run along its route. A line of forts and defenses had earlier been

The first military railroad of the Civil War was built by the Confederacy, a 5.5-mile spur off the Orange and Alexandria Railroad near Manassas Junction, Virginia. (*Library of Congress*)

built along the countryside with substantial fortifications at the Centreville Plateau. The Centreville Road, along which provisions that had been moved from the supply base at Manassas Junction, had been trampled into a worthless mired mess by ox drawn wagons, thus the need for the railroad.

It was a rustic affair using old light rail— some of it pilfered from the B&O. Ties were spaced at roughly twice the normal length and no ballast was used. The railroad was used strictly for supplying food for the 40,000 Confederate troops at winter quarters in Centreville.

The line was abandoned in March 1861 when Confederates withdrew from defensive positions on the Centreville Plateau. They then moved south of the Rappahannock River to resist Union advances by Major General George McClellan. Confederates wrecked as much of the line as possible, destroying the trestle over Bull Run and tearing up much of the rail along the route.

The American Civil War was the first war fully documented through photography. The people back home, far from the battlefield, were able to get a graphic look at events. Out of tens of thousands of photographs taken during the war, nearly a thousand depict the railroad and its operations. Today we can examine other views of the war more closely and extract even more railroad subjects.

Both the North and South employed photographers to record nearly every aspect of the war. The "wet plate" collodion process was the standard of the day. Developed by Englishman Scott Archer, the process produced a negative on a glass plate using collodion, a thick liquid made by dissolving nitrated cotton in a mixture of ether and alcohol. The collodion, filled with light-sensitive salts such as potassium iodide, was then spread evenly across the plate. The ether and alcohol evaporated, leaving a film of iodides attached to the plate, which was then immersed in a solution of silver nitrates.

The photographer had to work fast. After taking his photo the plate had to be immediately developed before the solution dried, giving the process the term "wet collodion." Photographers could now produce numerous high-quality prints from the negative.

The most popular print was the stereo view—or stereograph. Using a camera with two lenses, the image was reproduced twice, slightly offset. When viewed through a stereo viewer, a dramatic three-dimensional effect was produced.

At a time when families invited guests over for nightly entertainments that might

The camera, railroad, and telegraph came of age during the war. Both sides employed professional photographers to document nearly every aspect of the conflict. Southern photographer Sam A. Cooley stands to the right of his camera in an expressive image of his crew and equipment. The wet-plate collodion process was the standard of the day. Many images were processed as stereographs. The wet-plate process, in the hands of professional photographers, often captured amazing detail. (*Library of Congress*)

include singing around the piano, parlor games such as charades, and having small musicals or plays performed, they could now enjoy the modern wonder of viewing stereo views. This led to lively discussions about the world and current events.

Americans in the 1860s lived in a world steeped in romanticism that would collide harshly with brutal reality. Photographs of dead soldiers strewn across battlefields, emaciated prisoners at Andersonville Prison, and cities pounded into rubble drew gasps. Images of heroism were thrilling. This was

no less the case with railroad images depicting massive rail facilities, highly adorned locomotives, rail-borne mortars, derailed trains, burned bridges, and scorched locomotives laying within the wreckage of demolished train sheds.

Numerous amateur photos survive but those taken by skilled professional photographers using superior equipment retain astonishing detail and clarity. The photos were often composed. A rail crew, for example, would be arranged around a locomotive and asked to retain a prideful and expressive pose for the long exposure. Any movement created a blurry ghost-like effect. But it is in some of the random, unstaged photos that we experience the emotions of the war.

A particularly poignant image of captured Union soldiers was taken on June 28, 1862, by photographer James Gibson after the Battle of Savage's Station, during the Peninsula Campaign (*see page 46*). In March 1862, Union General George B. McClellan attempted to end the war by capturing Richmond, the Confederate capital. General Lee was brought into the fight. In spite of his own blunders he aggressively attacked and out-maneuvered McClellan, driving Union forces away from Richmond and slugging them back up the Virginia Peninsula. During this lengthy campaign over 200,000 soldiers would engage in a series of six major engagements known as the Seven Days Battles, including Savage's Station. Combined casualties were over 26,000. The field hospital in Gibson's photograph was established in the yard around the Savage homestead not far from the Richmond & York River station. (This railroad provided service between Richmond and West Point, Virginia—a shipping port at the head of the York River. The western terminus was not far from Richmond's Tobacco Row. The line was a vital link during the Peninsular Campaign and would end up being largely destroyed.) The wounded soldiers depicted were part of 500 abandoned by McClellan, an action for which he would later be roundly criticized.

Deep within the image is a young soldier with his hand to his head. Clearly suffering, the soldier lying beside him appears to be tending to him, perhaps giving words of comfort and encouragement. Another photograph shows some of these Yankee wounded being evacuated on Richmond & York River flatcars to medical facilities at White House Landing.

Railroad fever swept across America starting in the 1830s. Railroads took up the adventure of opening the interior of the continent already underway by riverboats and canals. Early locomotives were imported from Europe but the *DeWitt Clinton* was one of the nation's first attempts at this new technology. Much of the locomotive was forged at the West Point Foundry in Cold Springs, New York. It began operations in 1831, running its curious stagecoach-styled cars on the Mohawk & Hudson Railroad. This is a reproduction of that famous locomotive and train built from the original plans. (*Library of Congress*)

There was plenty of experimentation in the early days. The *Uncle Tom*—most likely named after Harriet Beecher Stowe's character—seems disproportionate but not without charm. It features some interesting ornamentation such as a cast rooster on the sandbox, a hand painted landscape under the cab window and a cast iron black post boy on the pilot beam. (*Author's Collection*)

Early competition led to adorning locomotives to get customers' attention. In the case of the *Hackensack* there may have been accesses. Proud builders could not resist decorating their creations with intricate wrought iron bell and lamp holders, polished brass attachments, and beautiful hand painted scrollwork. This rather fragile appearing locomotive was built by Rogers in 1860 for the Hackensack & New York Railroad. (*Author's Collection*)

Immediately after the first shots were fired in the Civil War, both sides mobilized their railroads. The *E. M. Stanton*—named after Lincoln's Secretary of War—represents the modern, more powerful machines that would be put through brutal service. Built by Philadelphia builder, R. Norris and Son, the 4-6-0 poses grandly on a turntable. (*Library of Congress*)

The South could boast of some prestigious ante-bellum railroads built to service a primarily agricultural economy. Early southern innovations had an impact on the overall development of railroad technology in America. The forlorn condition of this equipment does, however, show the general state of many of their lines prior to the war. (*Author's Collection*)

The sense of organization and apparent endless supply of materials to service the North's railroads, depicted in this image at the USMRR yards in Alexandria, Virginia, was undoubtedly discouraging to the Confederacy but they found ways to try to even the score. (*Library of Congress*)

Neither side expected the war to escalate to the horrid dimensions it did. It was to be a quick "gentlemen's" war, to be over in mere months. These images of the massive destruction of the Manassas Junction rail facilities during the Rebel retreat in March 1862 would become commonplace. (*Library of Congress*)

Another view at Manassas was taken from the end of the turntable. Railroads would escalate, expand, and prolong the conflict, leading to much of its slaughter. War became unrestrained; capable of being projected anywhere rails could be laid. (*Library of Congress*)

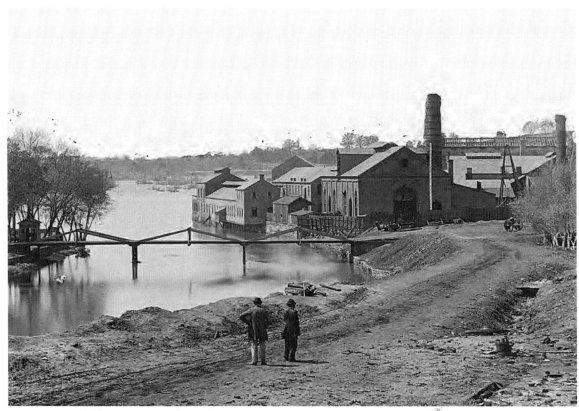

Tredegar Iron Works located at Richmond, Virginia, had much to do with that city being chosen as the Confederate Capital. It was the South's largest iron works, producing railroad equipment, cannon, munitions, and plating for ironclads. It employed up to 2,500 workers by 1863 and required constant military protection. The capitals of Richmond and Washington, DC, were only 105 miles apart and were much fought over. (*Library of Congress*)

Tredegar produced locomotives on a limited scale. The *Roanoke* was one of their early accomplishments, built in 1854 for the Virginia & Tennessee Railroad. The average age of southern locomotives seeing service in the war was ten years old. The *Roanoke* looks sturdy, sensible, balanced, and well machined. The outside frame with handrails make it handsome as do the proportioned balloon stack and cow catcher-used for tossing cattle off to the side. The train is sitting on strap-iron track—wood stringers topped with long strips of iron. (*Author's Collection*)

A bizarre and flamboyant sign displays examples of products offered by Archer McLeish Vulcan Iron Works of Charleston, South Carolina. Incorporated into the sculptural advertisement is one of their railroad products; "Dbl. Action Locomotive Springs." (*Library of Congress*)

Competition between the Confederate navy and railroads for iron continued throughout the war. The rustic *Albemarle* was built in a cornfield by a nineteen-year-old Confederate marine engineer using local carpenters and blacksmiths. It was an ironclad ram utilizing 4-inch-thick iron plates and a heavily reinforced bow for ramming enemy vessels. With it low draft, it prowled North Carolina's Albemarle Sound and waterways. Two Brook guns mounted on pivot carriages together with its powerful ramming capabilities proved deadly to wooden Union blockade ships. (*Author's Collection*)

This frail relic with its Pioneer style boiler was used on the Orange & Alexandria Railroad in Virginia during the war. There appears to be some kind of ramshackle fortification used for protecting the railroad in the upper right. Overall, the image captures the dusty, rural day-to-day operation of mid-1800s railroading. (*Library of Congress*)

Contraband workers are building a barricade around the vital Federal controlled Orange & Alexandria rail-head at Alexandria, Virginia, to protect it from destructive Confederate raids. The O&A would take a pounding from both sides during the war. Contraband was a term used during the Civil War for escaped slaves and others who came under command of Union forces. (*National Archives*)

When it became obvious the war was to be a prolonged affair, waterfront bases were quickly developed. Otherwise modest port towns were transformed into some of the busiest ports on earth. Troops along with tons of supplies arrived around the clock by steam and sailing vessels. The towering masts of schooners loom over a train dutifully bringing loaded supplies for Union troops up from the wharf at City Point, Virginia. (*Library of Congress*)

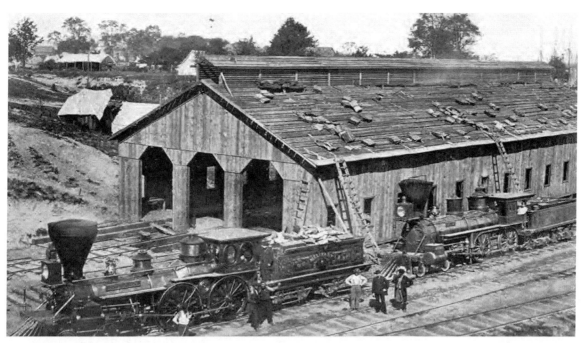

City Point would experience rapid development that left townsfolk unsettled. Here workers are finishing the roof on a new engine house. Federal personnel pose beside two USMRR locomotives. Eventually City Point would be expanded to supply Grant's army later in the war. (*Library of Congress*)

A portrait of Daniel Craig McCallum, superintendent of United States Military Rail Roads sits at the center of artwork emblazoned across the Mason-built tender of the locomotive dedicated to him. Some of this artwork included bold patriotic colors and gold leaf. (*Library of Congress*)

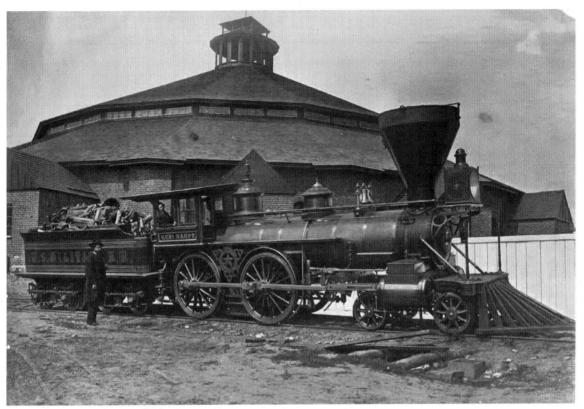

The locomotive *Genl. Haupt* poses outside the massive covered Orange & Alexandria roundhouse at Alexandria, in 1863. It too is a modern, sleek Mason-built machine with Russian iron boiler jacket and brass boiler bands. William Mason, a master builder, insisted on only the highest quality materials. His designs were uncluttered with needless decoration. He was an early industrial artist with an eye for balance and composition. Even the driver counter weights are inside the wheels, out of sight, so as to not interrupt the visual flow of the machine. It is certain Herman Haupt was proud to have his name on it. (*Library of Congress*)

An interesting transition is presented here. USMRR engines at Alexandria occupy the foreground. In the center are buildings associated with the Alexandria slave trade. The light colored buildings in the upper part of the photograph are barracks built for African American soldiers fighting for the Union. (*National Archives*)

The Firefly locomotive poses for a photograph atop an Orange & Alexandria bridge near Union Mills, Virginia. Confederates had destroyed the original bridge. Officials of the USMRR were not as concerned with the picturesque aspects of the location as they were in showing off their bridge building skills. (*Library of Congress*)

A rustic example along the road of locomotive evolution was the *Rein Deer*, built c.1850 by John Souther for the New Hampshire Railroad. It was an internal drive machine with uncertain bulky proportions. There is a winter landscape painted on the fender skirt and the cab is built with horizontal boards. (*Author's Collection*)

The majority of locomotives in service on both sides of the conflict were wood burners. It was common to have a "wood passer" in the tender to hand wood to the fireman. This powerful anthracite coal burner rolled from the Rogers erecting shops in 1863 and saw service on the New Jersey Railroad & Transportation Company. (*Author's Collection*)

The Baltimore & Ohio was the most important railroad involved in the defense of Washington and was therefore repeatedly savaged. It was a prestigious, well-managed line. The Grafton station and hotel at Grafton, Virginia (later West Virginia) was described in an 1857 newspaper as having "parlors gorgeously furnished. . . scenery grand and sublime. . . one of the institutions of the country." (*Library of Congress*)

The B&O facilities at Grafton would be involved in military operations particularly in 1862. The round-house is prominent in this Civil War-era photo. The combination station and hotel in the previous photo can be seen, less grandly, left of center. (*Library of Congress*)

Two USMRR engines, the *Genl. Dix* (left) and *Genl. McClellan*, run supplies and troops to Grant's headquarters along the James River in the vicinity of City Point, Virginia. The round Sibley tents provide shelter for officials and members of the Construction Corps—a vital arm of the USMRR. (*National Archives*)

Most photographs were staged, requiring human subjects to remain motionless for the duration of the exposure. An exception is this image taken by James Gibson of Union wounded in the yard of a field hospital
near Savage's Station, Virginia. It was taken in late June 1862 during the Seven Days Battles. General
McClellan had abandoned the soldiers as the Union withdrew. (*Library of Congress*)

Top, deep within the previous image is this scene of soldierly compassion. A suffering young soldier with a hand to his face appears to be comforted by the soldier beside him. Below, some of the Union wounded from the Battle of Savage's Station are being transported on the Richmond & York River railroad to a Federal hospital at White House Landing. (*National Archives*)

The newly completed Long Bridge would bear the travel of thousands of troops and trains. It was built within 100 feet of the old bridge and, like its predecessor, had swing sections on both ends to allow the passage of river traffic. (*Library of Congress*)

TWO

RAILS ACROSS THE POTOMAC

Confederacy. A League or compact for mutual support or common action.
—*Merriam-Webster Dictionary*

Last ditch efforts by delegates and fawning gestures to keep open rebellion from fanning into war failed in the spring of 1861. In early April Confederate batteries bombarded Fort Sumter in Charleston Harbor. There was no turning back. Yet there was a naive sense that hostilities would not last long. Federal enlistments, numbering 75,000, were issued for a mere 90 days. There was an air of adventure to the thing, if not outright excitement. But it would turn out the bitter contentiousness of decades-long regional tensions and economic injustices ran much deeper than believed.

West Point had been turning out reasonably adequate generals, some with brilliance and instinctual aptitudes beyond their instructors. But none were ready for what was to come. The battlefield would become a bloody confused classroom of unimagined carnage as modern industrial forces overwhelmed old theories of warfare. Even the most pessimistic men—those who instantly discarded noble thoughts of a quick, romantic war—could not have imagined the catastrophic blood-letting that lay ahead.

Washington, DC, had a modest population of around 2,000 citizens in the city proper, many of whom left for the countryside during the humid hot summer months. Things were about to change. Panic set in when Confederates tried to capture the city and make it their capital. A railroad circumventing Baltimore, supervised by Andrew Carnegie, was hastily constructed to rush in troops to fend off the Confederate assault on April 25.

Defended only by a single fort—rickety old Fort Washington about a dozen miles south of the city—dread gripped Washingtonians. With hopes that the war would be over after one decisive strike, Federal troops were sent on the offensive to take the Confederate capital at Richmond, Virginia. To do this they first had to secure the important rail facilities at Manassas Junction, Virginia, about 30 miles southwest of Washington. On July 21, 1861, while in pursuit of this target, Union and Confederate forces clashed at Bull Run. The battle resulted in a stunning defeat for the North.

This was to be no quick gentleman's war. Lincoln, realizing the nation was now in for a lengthy conflict, immediately ordered durable fortifications for Washington, DC. In August 1861, he organized the Department of the Potomac and the Army of the Potomac.

The population of Washington swelled as troops and officials were hurried in. Anguished Washingtonians were only too happy to welcome them and protection wasn't the only thing on their minds. Along with the clatter of wagon trains, saw mills rendering lumber, and the gritty swoosh of masons' trowels slathering mortar between bricks came the sweetly silent prospects for vast profits. There was something calming about the latter, even to those who sympathized with the South. It produced a boon. Warehouses, departmental offices, stockyards, barracks, hotels, and hospitals sprang up everywhere.

On April 16, 1862, slavery was abolished in the city—eight months before Lincoln's Emancipation Proclamation. Freed slaves applied for employment in the massive defense projects. The Department of the Potomac, under the command of Major General George B. McClellan, quickly surrounded the city with 33 miles of fortifications, entrenchments, and nearly 70 forts situated along the heights. Cannon with barrels aiming southward and stepped-up gunboats patrolling the river did much to dissuade further assaults by an emboldened Confederacy. The capital had become one of the most heavily defended cities in history.

In 1808, President Thomas Jefferson signed an act of Congress allowing construction of the Long Bridge to connect Alexandria, Virginia, to the detached section of the new capital. Crossings to the seat of power had previously been made by often-dangerous ferry trips. Rural carpenters erected the crude span. Their limited understanding of such ambitious bridge construction—especially one with draw spans—did not interfere with the finished project becoming an object of national pride. Its stature increased when the British damaged it during the War of 1812.

In 1846, President James K. Polk restored Alexandria back to the state of Virginia. The fervently expansionist Baltimore & Ohio Railroad, which had been providing service to Washington, DC, from the north since 1835, tried to arrange a deal with the Alexandria & Washington Railroad to put tracks across Long Bridge. An appeal to the Virginia legislature, promising substantial improvements to the bridge was denied. Railroads would have to continue to unload cargo at the approaches to the bridge and transport it along the mile-long span with horse- or mule-drawn wagons.

Lincoln's fortification of Washington did not ignore the importance of Long Bridge. Rails were laid across the crude span but only freight cars were allowed to cross and they were to be towed by horses. As an added precaution, the freight had to be evenly distributed within the cars. Armed guards were stationed at the approaches.

Upon formation of the United States Military Rail Roads, Lincoln ignored Alexandria's prior restoration to Virginia and sent forces to capture the city. Virginia's secession from the Union on May 23, 1861, made this doubly important. The significant Orange & Alexandria Railroad facilities there would prove especially useful when joined with lesser regional railroads. The Union and Confederate capitals were a mere 105 miles apart. Both sides reasoned that a deathblow to their opponent's seat of power would bring victory.

With Washington roughly three miles from the water's edge and rail traffic across the Potomac minimal, it was necessary to set up USMRR headquarters at the O&A facilities. Construction of another more sturdy Long Bridge to handle the heavy wartime railroad traffic was soon undertaken. Located about 100 feet down river from the original span, it would not be completed until 1863. Until then, USMRR operations would have to be launched from Alexandria.

Always considered one of America's most beautiful cities, Alexandria was an important port of entry since the 1650s. Sadly, it had always known war. General Washington drilled troops there in 1754. It was a base during the French and Indian War and was captured and ransomed by the British in the War of 1812.

The city held and sold slaves but it was also home to several free black communities. African Americans in these neighborhoods participated in some of Alexandria's important social institutions and were generally welcomed by whites. African American artisans flourished.

Under Union military occupation, escaped slaves from other regions poured in. Although still considered property prior to emancipation, they were labeled contraband which prohibited them from being returned to their owners. The Federal government both in Alexandria and Washington enthusiastically employed them.

The nucleus of the USMRR was quickly developed at the Orange & Alexandria yards. On May 24, 1861, Federal troops seized control of the main terminal, roundhouse, machines shops, and two locomotives. Retreating Confederates wrecked 22 miles of O&A track and bridges between Cameron Run and Fairfax Station.

The O&A was chartered in 1848 to run from Alexandria to Gordonville. The first line was completed in 1854 with a connection to the Virginia Central Railroad over which it had to pay trackage rights. In 1860 an extension was completed between Charlottesville and Lynchburg with connections to the Virginia & Tennessee Railroad and the South Side Railroad. It was now an intrastate system and would become one the most fought over railroads in the war.

Chaos reigned in lines south of Washington during the summer and fall of 1861. Confederate raiders were fast at work disrupting border state lines by destroying miles of track, bridges, and equipment to hold back Union forces. As many as 40 fine locomotives in use on the Baltimore and Ohio had been destroyed by burning, wrecking using crowbars and hammers, or by plunging them into the Potomac. Twenty-three B&O bridges were destroyed including the impressive span over the Potomac at Harpers Ferry.

Much of first year's fighting occurred in Virginia. Confederates burned federally held wharves and storage buildings at Aquia Creek as well as bridges across the Potomac and the Rappahannock rivers.

Lincoln, having militarized all railroads in the eastern war zone, again strongly urged other lines to support the war effort or face

Daniel Craig McCallum, left, emigrated from Scotland with his parents in 1815 and grew up in Rochester, New York. His educational pursuits included architecture and engineering. As superintendent of the New York & Erie Railroad, he developed an interest in bridge design. He formed his McCallum Bridge Company where he did well with his patented Arched Truss Bridge. He was appointed superintendent of United States Rail Roads in February 1862. A brilliant engineer and steadfast leader, he successfully oversaw most of the USMRR operations. Herman Haupt, right, West Point educated with a bend towards engineering, proved an admirable assistant to McCallum. He preferred being out in the field where McCallum was more of a deskman. He had little patience for pompous generals and let them know it. Intelligent, creative, and determined, he could instantly assess a situation and develop a course of action. (*Library of Congress*)

Federal takeover. He believed civilians should run the railroads, especially since they knew better than military men how to run them.

Daniel Craig McCallum and Herman Haupt were commissioned to oversee operations of the USMRR. Scottish born McCallum was an architect, engineer, and poet. He invented an arched bridge truss that became so successful he used it to develop his own McCallum Bridge Company. That, together with lucrative railroad consultant fees, made him quite the entrepreneur.

Herman Haupt was born into a prosperous Philadelphia family. He attended private schools and then graduated from West Point in 1835 at age 18. After a stint in the military he turned his footsteps to the challenge of railroad engineering. Briefly he departed to teach mathematics at Pennsylvania College in Gettysburg but was soon lured back to railroading, becoming superintendent of the recently formed Pennsylvania Railroad. Ever restless, he resigned in 1856 and immersed himself in his greatest civilian endeavor, construction of the Hoosac Tunnel. He was hard at work on it when Secretary of War, Edwin M. Stanton, commissioned him to help supervise the new Federal railroad system. He responded when his country called, leaving his supervision of construction of the Hoosac Tunnel. He would be dogged with lawsuits from the controlling interests of that project and would suffer financially. Stanton and Lincoln could not have done better in securing Haupt's services. Originally Stanton brought him in for temporary service during the Peninsula Campaign primarily to oversee repairs to damaged bridges and track on the Aquia Creek & Fredericksburg Railroad. The commission was to last about a month but Haupt would end up staying with the USMRR until September 1863, when he got into a disagreement with Stanton and was relieved.

The methods utilized by Herman Haupt and Daniel Craig McCallum in crippling Southern railroads ranged from simple to labor intensive. Haupt was a man unimpressed by military rank and may have delighted in pulling a general or two off his emotional high horse. He delivered orders with the directness of a stream of tobacco juice aimed furiously at a saloon spittoon.

He insisted on three fundamental rules:

1. Not to allow supplies to be forwarded to the advanced terminus until they are actually required, and only in such quantities as can be promptly removed.

2. To insist on prompt unloading and return of cars.

3. To permit no delays of trains beyond the time fixed for starting, but when necessary and practicable, to furnish extras, if the proper accommodation of business required it.

Overall Haupt worked well with McCallum who, despite being his supervisor, pretty much gave him free rein. McCallum was more a deskman where Haupt preferred the field. Haupt's greatest contribution was organizing the Construction Corp of the United States Military Rail Roads. The corps laid the groundwork for railroad utilization in future wars.

The war effort resulted in enormous government contracts for rail, lumber, rolling stock, and construction or outright purchase of hundreds of locomotives. In spite of this, McCallum warned railroad companies that price gouging would result in Federal shops being built thus pushing the private sector out of the action.

Although the needs of the USMRR would expand significantly, its ultimate purpose would be to support General Grant in his strategy to defeat General Lee's Army of Northern Virginia during the Siege of Petersburg. Over 100,000 troops, more than

65,000 horses and mules, and tons of provisions would be supplied from the Federal base at City Point, Virginia. Dozens of schooners and steamboats arrived daily at the eight newly constructed wharves. The USMRR Construction Corps would build nearly 300 structures by the end of the siege. Many of the structures were prefabricated—the lumber being precut to specifications and then assembled upon arrival at the port.

The railroad followed Grant as he arrayed his forces around Petersburg, the immediate terrain being surveyed for additional spurs. Twenty-one miles of railroad were laid over which 25 locomotives using 275 pieces of rolling stock would traverse around the clock. Nearly two and a half million miles would be logged. Stations were erected where needed. Sidings and run around tracks were laid to allow uninterrupted mainline through traffic. Timetables and other logistical considerations ran remarkably smoothly. All of this would ultimately lead to Lee's defeat in Virginia.

Early accomplishments under Haupt and McCallum included restoring railroad service to Fredericksburg, Virginia. During the first year of the war The Richmond, Fredericksburg & Potomac Railroad provided supplies to Confederate encampments and posts along the Potomac. In the spring of 1862, General Joseph E. Johnston ordered his Confederate troops to abandon the region. During their withdrawal they destroyed RF&P tracks and the trestle spanning the Potomac Creek.

In May 1862, Herman Haupt went to work restoring the track and bridge. Nagging rain and scarcity of materials made the going tough. Amazingly, three miles of track would

USMRR Construction Corps rebuilding the Orange & Alexandria Railroad bridge over Cedar Run near Catlett's Station, Virginia, in 1863. (*Library of Congress*)

be laid in only three days and a bridge over Ackakee Creek—a span 120 feet long and 30 feet high—would be built in 15 hours.

It was the trestle over Potomac Creek, however, that would raise emotions in the surrounding counties. The wrecked antebellum bridge had taken nine months to build. Confederate General Joseph E. Johnston's troops had collapsed it into the creek during their withdrawal from the district. Herman Haupt supervised relatively unskilled infantrymen in construction of the new trestle. Built in only nine days, it would bear not only normal but also steadily increasing train traffic. The countryside was bludgeoned as over two million board feet of neighboring lumber was hastily hacked and sawn. The supports comprising much of the open crib-work were not even striped of their bark.

During a visit to the Fredericksburg area,

President Lincoln, Secretary Stanton, and Rear Admiral John A. Dahlgren ventured to the area to see the trestle. Lincoln led the other two men on a harrowing walk across the 80-foot high, 400-foot long span. Stanton found the experience unnerving, becoming dizzy to the point that he had to grasp Dahlgren's hand to complete the journey.

After the visit, Lincoln reflected on the day's experience, being amused at the rustic quality of the bridge:

I have seen the most remarkable structure that human eyes ever rested upon. That man Haupt has built a bridge across Potomac Creek, almost 400 feet long and 100 feet high, over which loaded trains are running ever hour, and, upon my word, gentlemen, there is nothing in it but beanpoles and corn-stalks.

During the course of the next three years Union troops would build four bridges atop the stone abutments, such was the action in that district.

The intensity of railroad activity at the onset of the war would only increase. Railroads would be destroyed and rebuilt as many as five times in some cases. When Confederate troops retreated they tore up rails, burned bridges and water towers. They moved what engines and rolling stock they could, sometimes moving engines overland on reinforced wagons. What couldn't be moved was burned, disabled, or rolled into rivers. Armies continued to grow in size from the earlier contests. Railroads had clearly changed the face of war.

The USMRR Construction Corps quickly rebuilt miles of wrecked track. Retreating forces were not their only problem. Confederate partisan raiders made life a living hell for Union railroad men.

Among these partisans were highly trained cavalrymen who rumbled out from their secluded camps and viciously attacked Union held railroads and wagon trains, often returning with much needed food and supplies for desperate Confederate troops.

Turner Ashby, John S. Mosby, and John H. Morgan led the three most famous of these independent partisan bands. Ashby's daring exploits took on mythical proportions. A dashing man with a long beard, he rode a magnificent white horse, which he sometimes brought in sight of Union soldiers. He would stand beside the horse on a hill or rise and taunt the enemy, striking a pose brimming with southern gallantry. As Union soldiers approached, he'd casually ride off and then stop again, affecting a similar pose,

Turning raiders against Union-held railroads was one way Confederate President Davis countered the onslaught of the USMRR. Turner Ashby was among the elite. His raiders were superb cavalrymen who lunged from the woods on savage attacks against railroads. Using small field pieces and tools easily carried on their horses, they could quickly tear up rail, burn ties, bring down telegraph lines, burn cars, and disable locomotives. Ashby's raiders were particularly effective in hampering Union railroad activity in northern Virginia. (*Library of Congress*)

almost like the beckoning of the ghost on the ramparts of the castle in *Hamlet*. The attacks Ashby led became legend. His heroics did much to lift the spirits of Southern soldiers as they sat around the campfire. The Union put him at the top of the list of who they wanted captured or killed.

Raiders integrated various methods for derailing trains. This included putting obstructions on the track or removing spikes from a length of rail so the train would jump off the track. They skillfully disabled locomotives and burned rolling stock. Their objectives went beyond just destruction, however. They would raid an isolated telegraph office along a rail line, tie up the operator, and listen in on Federal communications—sometimes for hours at a time. Using their own telegraph operator, they would connect their portable telegraph machine into Federal communications, sending misinformation and false orders to further jam operations.

There were other independent raider groups whose modes of guerrilla warfare left a trail of blood and destruction around Union controlled railroads. Sometimes called jayhawkers and bushwhackers, they were fearless in their daring assaults.

Not to be outdone, Herman Haupt took revenge on southern railroads with his own cavalry unit, but did so without Ashby's theatrics. He produced a manual with detailed instructions and pasted-in photographs showing how to disable track in a matter of minutes. Since heavy tools could not be carried, special instruments were devised that allowed his raiders to pull up rails. He also blew up southern bridges with a new device he called the torpedo. An auger was used to drill holes in the bridge's supporting timbers and cross members. Eight-inch torpedoes, packed with gunpowder, were pressed in the holes and then their two-foot long fuses were lit. Many Confederate bridges collapsed into smoldering wrecks using this technique.

For disabling locomotives, Haupt patiently considered recommendations but as far as he was concerned nothing worked better than a canon ball through the boiler. As for wrecking rolling stock, fire was the way to go. Haupt figured his elite cavalry had, by war's end, destroyed over 400 cars.

The war's violence soon burst from the caldron between the two capitals, plunging deeper south, westward, and north. Whenever the Billy Yank landed a punch, Johnny Reb would usually counter with a bruising punch of his own. The railroad tore through the limitations of traditional warfare as never before. Anywhere there were rails a battle could occur. Armies could now be supplied from bases hundreds of miles away. War could be waged across the width and breadth of America.

The tradition of armies massing to annihilate each other became increasingly difficult with this new rapid mobility. Often armies were left chasing each other in circles across the countryside. The focus then became the severing of the enemy's rail supply lines in hopes of cornering him for a chance at destruction.

Cities fed by numerous railroads were not the only targets. Small peaceable towns beyond the railheads were the sites of the bloodiest engagements. Gettysburg and Antietam are among the most notable. The likelihood of a decisive war-ending battle grew less likely. Instead there were hundreds of battles, large and small, leading to massive casualties.

The railroads often worked in conjunction with navy vessels to transport troops and supplies to battle sites. Gallant riverboats on both sides transported men from one port to another where trains took them inland. First Manassas was an example of an important battle that developed around a remote railroad junction. Bowling Green in Kentucky and Corinth in Mississippi were others. All three occurred in the first year of the war.

Kentucky, a slave holding state, had declared neutrality in the war but this did not lessen President Lincoln's anguish over the pivotal state. At first both sides courted Kentucky but then resorted to torment by intruding on their neutrality as early as the summer of 1861. The state lay along the northern border of Tennessee and provided access to the Ohio and Mississippi Rivers. Lincoln's attention to Kentucky went beyond it being his birthplace (and Mary Todd's and Jefferson Davis's as well). His fear that the bluegrass state might swing towards the Confederate States of America made him lament:

> I think to lose Kentucky is nearly the same as to lose the whole game. Kentucky gone, we cannot hold Missouri, nor, as I think Maryland. These all against us, the job on our hands is too large for us. We would as well consent to separation at once, including the surrender of the capital.

Along with its natural resources Kentucky had a growing industrial base. Caught in the spasms of war right from the start, it had its own political deformities tearing it apart. Slaves comprised 19 percent of the population, something most pro-Union Kentuckians could live with. Governor Beriah Magoffin believed in the rights of states to secede but still tried, unsuccessfully, to mediate deals to keep the union together—peacefully. He nonetheless responded tersely to a telegraph sent by Lincoln on April 15, 1861, requesting Kentuckians be included in the 75,000 troops assembling to quell the rebellion:

> President Lincoln, Washington, DC. I will send not a man nor a dollar for the wicked purpose of subduing my sister Southern states. B. Magoffin.

Kentucky would be scene to some of the most brutal battles of the war. The Confederacy desperately wanted its industrial power and fought hard to win it. In a special congressional election held June 20, 1861, Unionist candidates won nine of ten congressional seats leading to veto-proof majorities in the House and Senate. Politically the state was now tilted towards the Union column. It was a devastating blow to the Confederacy but they were not going to give up easily.

Politically fractured Kentucky was a state where the term "brother fighting brother" would become literal. Its fragile neutrality was violated September 4, 1861, when Confederate General Leonidas Polk ordered Brigadier General Gideon Johnson Pillow to occupy Columbus and take control of the important Mobile & Ohio Railroad terminus. The M&O was chartered in 1848 by the states of Alabama, Kentucky, Mississippi, and Tennessee with a projected route between the Gulf seaport of Mobile, Alabama, and the Ohio River near Cairo, Illinois. The entire railroad was the target of both sides during the war and would be left in near ruin at the end.

The Union responded September 6 by sending Brigadier General Ulysses S. Grant into Paducah, Kentucky, where he seized control of the northern end of the New Orleans & Ohio Railroad and part of the Tennessee River. Now in the thick of it, Kentucky's General Assembly ordered the Confederates to leave the state. When the

Lookout Mountain looms over war-time Chattanooga, Tennessee. Note the arched roof of the railroad shed, left center. (*National Archives*)

order was ignored the Assembly had the Union flag raised over the capital in Frankfort. Allegiance to the Union was sealed.

Aggressive Confederate activities continued under Albert Sidney Johnston who assembled a defense line in the trans-Allegheny west extending from Columbus to Bowling Green and then to Cumberland Gap. Stretching over 400 miles, it could not possibly be maintained. Grant, using his forces accompanied by gunboats on the Tennessee River, broke through it in February. With the rail junction at Bowling Green captured, Johnston withdrew to Corinth, Mississippi, where the Memphis & Charleston Railroad crossed the Mobile & Ohio. He remained there while his troop

strength was reinforced from men brought in on both rail lines. The two railroads were the largest in the South—the M&O being especially significant in that it was the only east-west route. Corinth was incorporated in 1853 as Cross City to reflect the importance of the junction of the two railroads, but local newspaper editor, W. E. Gibson thought the place should have a more classical name and suggested Corinth after the historic cross-roads city in ancient Greece.

Johnston and Grant clashed on April 6, 1862, at Shiloh Church. Johnston was killed the first day. During the night Grant was reinforced with troops from the Army of the Ohio. Confederate General P. G. T. Beauregard replaced Johnston. He was a skillful general but Grant pounded him back during the next day's fighting. A high price was paid. The two days of bloodletting at Shiloh resulted in over 23,000 combined casualties.

Beauregard withdrew his defeated army back to Corinth. Pursued by Union Major General Henry W. Halleck, Beauregard was forced to abandon the city, moving his troops on to Tupelo, Mississippi, on the M&O. Another battle to take control of Corinth would be fought by different armies on October 3-4.

Beauregard asked to be relieved of command due to health problems shortly after Shiloh. He was replaced with General Braxton Bragg, an ill-natured fussbudget of a leader. As commander of the newly named Army of the Mississippi, he was determined to retake Tennessee and possibly Kentucky. His first challenge, however, was to thwart an attempt by Union forces under the command of Major General Ormsby M. Mitchel to take Chattanooga.

The Yanks were spotted moving along the Memphis & Charleston towards the city. The South simply could not allow Chattanooga to fall into Union hands. It was a vital railroad center providing rail transport and telegraph communications from the trans-Allegheny west to the Confederate capital at Richmond, Virginia.

What followed was a complex journey of brutal skirmishes and battles, of starving and thirsty soldiers marching in scorching heat, of foraging and rapacious attacks on supply depots—of dodges and deadly stumbles. The affair would include the largest transport of Confederate troops by rail in the war. Braxton Bragg ordered 30,000 soldiers to Chattanooga. Approximately 25,000 came by rail from Tupelo, Mississippi, to Mobile; then to Montgomery, Atlanta, and finally to Chattanooga. The timetables were tight and soldiers were prevented from seeking brothels during stay-overs.

All of this continued into 1863 and would change the course of the war. Bragg got control of Chattanooga. That, together with Lee's success at the First Manassas, inspired Southerners to believe they could prevail.

Bragg indeed took Chattanooga but couldn't hold it. He took central Tennessee for a time and almost got precious Kentucky but sympathetic pro-Confederate Kentuckians who promised to come to his aid betrayed him.

A thick mist over Lookout Mountain during the November 1863 battle led to the name, "The Battle Above the Clouds." Union troops would seize control of a junction of the Nashville & Trenton Railroad at Wauhatchie, which would provide food to starving troops in Chattanooga. On November 25, 1863, Union troops under the command of General George H. Thomas would charge Confederate rifle pits at Missionary Ridge.

General Ulysses S. Grant would take Orchard Knob with his Army of the Cumberland and then direct them against the seemingly impregnable fortifications atop Missionary Ridge, as would General Sherman when he arrived with his troops. Union forces prevailed. Now, with the Confederate's Army of Tennessee wrecked, Southerners' hopes once again waned.

These events are but a few of the complex maneuvers and actions around Chattanooga and demonstrate how railroads immediately expanded and affected the war, in this case to the Western Theater. Furthermore, Sherman would use the rail facilities at Chattanooga to launch his 1864 Atlanta Campaign and March to the Sea. Engines at Alexandria, Virginia, lettered USMRR, were already hissing and coughing, waiting to steam westward.

The famous story of the Andrews Raid (or Great Locomotive Chase) involved Chattanooga and so should be touched upon. Retold in books, songs, and movies, the raid remains the greatest railroad adventure of the war.

On April 12, 1862, Union volunteers directed by civilian scout and spy, James J. Andrews, embarked on a daring raid to destroy a portion of the Western & Atlantic's main stem between Atlanta and Chattanooga. The idea was to prevent Confederate troop reinforcements from Atlanta to reach Chattanooga. This would allow Union forces under the command of Major General Ormsby M. Mitchell to seize the latter.

On that morning of April 12, a passenger train pulled by the locomotive *General* was stopped at Big Shanty, Georgia, so passengers could have breakfast. This included the engineer and his crew. Andrews and his raiders hijacked the *General* and several railcars during this meal stop and steamed north towards Chattanooga. Along the way they planed to destroy track, bridges, and equipment while tearing down telegraph lines so stations ahead would not know they were coming.

The *General's* conductor, William Allen Fuller, looked on in horror as his engine rolled out of Big Shanty. He and two other crewmen chased the engine first on foot and then by handcar. At Etowah, Georgia, Fuller

and his men commandeered the *Yonah* and continued their chase north to Kingston. At Kingston they took control of the *William R. Smith* and steamed after their stolen train to within two miles of Adairsville. Andrews had wrecked the track here so Fuller and his men had to go it on foot the two miles to the town where they commandeered the southbound locomotive *Texas*.

With telegraph lines down stationmasters and crews up the line had no idea what was going on. The *Texas*, running in reverse, picked up 11 Confederates at Calhoun and continued the chase with the throttle open. The two trains steamed at high speeds across the Georgia countryside, racing through Dalton and Tunnel Hill.

Andrews continued to bring down telegraph lines but his plans to dynamite Tunnel Hill and burn bridges failed when the *General's* rain-soaked wood refused to burn. The locomotive stalled near Ringgold, just a few miles from Chattanooga. Andrews and his raiders abandoned the engine and bounded across the countryside. They were captured, along with two others who missed the raid by oversleeping. On June 7 Andrews was hanged in Atlanta. On June 18 seven other raiders were hanged. Eight raiders escaped from confinement and made it back to Union lines. This included two who were aided by slaves. Some of these men would receive the first Medals of Honor ever presented.

The defense of Washington, DC—called Washington City in those days—required use of the old Long Bridge across the Potomac. It was incapable of handling the heavy rail travel that would be needed between the capital and Alexandria, Virginia, so construction of a new bridge began immediately. The new bridge can be seen on the left. This old bridge, still important for foot travel, shows rails nearly buried from lack of use. (*National Archives*)

The new Long Bridge viewed from the Virginia side of the Potomac River. (*Library of Congress*)

Long Bridge was of course heavily guarded. Here soldiers pose with ordnance outside the hotel at the Washington approach to the bridge. There are several rows of rail suggesting different gauges could be accommodated. (*Library of Congress*)

The Orange & Alexandria Railroad facilities at Alexandria were seized early in the conflict. They became the base from which United States Military Rail Roads's operations were launched. This view is east, showing the O&A roundhouse, depot, and some yard trackage. The pole was used to elevate signal lanterns as traffic increased. (*Library of Congress*)

Early attempts by Confederates to capture Washington for their capital led to massive fortification of the city. Alexandria would be fortified as well. Guns of Battery Rogers at Hunting Creek peer out over the Potomac River from the Alexandria side. (*Library of Congress*)

A closer look at the previous image shows one of the enlarged Alexandria wharves fitted with rail to handle freight cars brought across the river on special barges. The tall signal towers were used to help railroad men guide barges into the wharf while keeping a close watch for any suspicious activity in the area. (*Library of Congress*)

The nearly completed dome of the Capitol is visible in this photo of locomotives and boxcars at the Maryland Street Washington & Alexandria depot. The short line with its simple station was suddenly of vast importance as it connected Washington, DC, with the Orange & Alexandria line. Hundreds of trains loaded with troops and supplies would traverse its 7-mile length. (*National Archives*)

The exquisite *J. H. Devereux* poses outside the O&A roundhouse in Alexandria. John H. Devereux was the superintendent of the Alexandria facilities. The engine, built by the New Jersey Locomotive & Machine Company in Paterson, New Jersey, had no equal in terms of decoration. Intricate wrought iron braces support the bell and headlamp. The sand dome has a portrait of Devereux. The drivers have hand painted scrollwork on the spokes and there is an elaborate fender plate. (*Library of Congress*)

The movable bridge sections on this Alexandria railroad wharf were engineered to align with the rails on barges so that cars could transfer easily. Noted photographer Andrew J. Russell took the photo. He was commissioned by the USMRR to document railroad operations. (*Library of Congress*)

The barges could transfer eight loaded cars without the time consuming process of unloading and reloading their freight. General Herman Haupt called them "floats" and was very satisfied with the ingenuity of the system. Two large Schuylkill barges were fastened together with large timbers arranged like long railroad ties. Rails were spiked to them and special braces would hold the cars in place for the crossing. Tugboats towed the barges between Alexandria and the base at Aquia Creek. Engines were also moved this way. (*Library of Congress*)

Trains take on supplies at City Point, Virginia, to move to the front. The small village became one of the busiest ports in the world virtually overnight. Wagon trains arrived daily along with hundreds of ships. (*National Archives*)

An example of Confederate raider activity is clearly evident in this c. 1863 image of the USMRR *Commodore*. The Construction Corps workers down the track have cleared wreckage from the track and repaired rail so through traffic can continue. (*Library of Congress*)

The damage to the *Commodore* is evident. The balloon stack, domes, cab, and tender have all been destroyed in the derailment. (*Author's Collection*)

The *Rapidan*, a powerful 4-6-O built in 1856 by the Virginia Locomotive and Car Works, has the task of bringing the *Commodore* back to Alexandria for repairs. Also in tow is the locomotive *Union*. The *Rapidan* had been seized early in the war. When Lincoln took the O&A shops at Alexandria, Confederate officials quickly withdrew 16 locomotives and a number of cars to Manassas to keep them out of Yankee hands, but the USMRR captured the *Rapidan*. (*Library of Congress*)

A closer look at the *Union* shows it was an older USMRR locomotive, probably purchased from a regional railroad in northern Virginia. The absence of its stack, domes and bell suggest it was a victim of Rebel activity. (*Library of Congress*)

An unidentified photographer and assistant enjoy a picnic along Bull Run in March of 1861. Behind them is the wreckage of the Centreville Military Railroad. The 5.5-mile railroad—essentially a spur off the O&A—was built by the Confederacy in November 1861. It was truly a rough affair, running east of Manassas Junction to the south side of the Centreville Plateau. Its purpose was to supply Gen. Joseph E. Johnston's Confederate Army of the Potomac. (*Library of Congress*)

Confederates destroyed the ante-bellum bridge carrying the Richmond, Fredericksburg & Potomac Railroad over Potomac Creek. Construction of this replacement bridge was supervised by Herman Haupt. Using unskilled infantrymen, he got it built in only nine days. It was a sensation, causing an astonished Lincoln to exclaim in his praise of it, "gentlemen, there is nothing in it but beanpoles and cornstalks." (*Library of Congress*)

The "beanpoles and cornstalks" bridge over Potomac Creek would be replaced in early 1863 with this more substantial span. The trusses were fabricated at Alexandria and brought here by train where the Construction Corps assembled them. (*National Archives*)

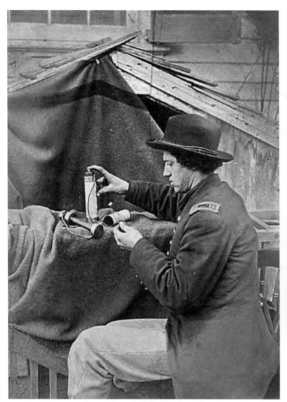 

A USMRR Construction Corps technician, left, prepares a "torpedo," a weapon developed to bring down bridges. Holes were drilled into bridge supports with an auger, right, and the torpedo was then pressed in. When everything was in place, the torpedo's fuse was lit. When done properly, a sturdy bridge would collapse in seconds. (*Library of Congress*)

The Great Locomotive Chase or Andrews' Raid remains the most famous train adventure of the war. On April 12, 1862, Union agents captured the locomotive *General* (shown in the 1880s after modifications) at Big Shanty, Georgia, and drove it at high speed on a destructive rampage up the Western & Atlantic Railroad towards Chattanooga. It was pursued by several Confederate locomotives, most notably, the *Texas*. Andrews and his raiders were captured; some were tried and later hanged, other languished in prison, while eight made daring escapes back to Union lines. Surviving raiders were the first recipients of the Medal of Honor. Both the *General* and the *Texas* were preserved and are located at museums in Atlanta. (*Author's Collection*)

The *John T. Souter* was nearly identical to the *General*. Both had outside supplementary frames but the General had a strap iron cowcatcher and larger drivers. Both locomotives were built by Rogers, Ketchum & Grosvenor of Patterson, New Jersey—the *Souter* for the Nashville & Chattanooga and the *General* for the Western & Atlantic. The *General* cost $8,850 in 1855. (*Author's Collection*)

The *Texas* was built in 1856 by Danforth, Cooke and Company in Paterson, New Jersey. It provided freight and passenger service on the Western & Atlantic prior to the war. During the Andrews' Raid, the locomotive was pulling a load of 21 cars towards Atlanta when it was commandeered by the stolen *General*'s conductor, William Allen Fuller, to make chase. The *Texas* pursued the *General* steaming in reverse. This photo shows the *Texas* after it underwent reworking after the war. (*Author's Collection*)

Union soldiers—no more than boys—stand guard over burned cars at Manassas Junction in this photo taken in August 1862 by Timothy H. O'Sullivan. Rebels had burned nearly 300 cars down to their wheels to keep them out of Union hands. The truck frames are cast iron sections bolted and riveted together. Segments of tin used to protect boxcar roofs lay between the trucks and rail. Note the bare feet of the soldier in the middle. (*Library of Congress*)

Boxcars on the Richmond & York River Railroad have brought in supplies to General McClellan's head-quarters at Savage Station, Virginia, during the Peninsula Campaign in 1862. The hard fought effort to take the Confederate Capital of Richmond was filled with ironies. The succession of battles were recorded as Union victories but Lee nonetheless drove the Union army away from Richmond and up the peninsula, causing them to flee on boats back to Alexandria. (*National Archives*)

An early style passenger car emblazoned with United States Military Rail Roads sits on a siding at City Point. Two Sibley tents and a wall tent are at the trackside. (*National Archives*)

A Confederate train steams away from the station at Corinth, Mississippi. The town was an important rail center and would be the scene of two battles. (*Library of Congress*)

This view shows the Tishomingo Hotel on the tracks at Corinth, Mississippi. The battles of Corinth 1 and 2, both occurring in 1862, involved the junction of the Mobile & Ohio and the Memphis & Charleston Railroads. (*Library of Congress*)

Block and tackle are being used to drag this USMRR locomotive back up the ravine it landed in after Rebels derailed it while chugging down the Manassas Gap Railroad. (*Author's Collection*)

A Federal railroad official displays a length of severely twisted rail. The method being demonstrated in the photograph involves a horse pulling a section of rail around a sturdy spike driven into a tie. In the foreground are tools used for this technique. They include an ax, auger, and sledgehammer. (*Library of Congress*)

A substantial Confederate earthwork fortification along the Orange & Alexandria line at Manassas, Virginia, is under Union control in this August 1862 photo. USMRR boxcars stand on the former Confederate rail supply line. (*Library of Congress*)

Top, White House Landing was located on the south shore of the Pamunkey River in New Kent County, Virginia. It was the site of a major Union supply base fed by the Richmond & York River Railroad. White House Plantation was home to Martha Dandridge Custis, wife of George Washington. There is a portable darkroom in the lower left corner of the photo. Bottom, an enlargement of the photograph reveals the elaborately decorated locomotive *U.S. Grant*. The oval cab windows were the work of an obviously skilled craftsman. (*National Archives*)

African American troops linger in a trampled camp in Chattanooga, Tennessee. The Union Army paid them at a lower rate than white soldiers. The loading platform in the foreground is along a "wye," a configuration of three tracks connected with switches used to turn trains around. (*Library of Congress*)

Top, a locomotive waits at the entrance of the massive train shed at Chattanooga. (*Author's Collection*)
Bottom, Confederate prisoners await trains that will take them to Union prisons. The scene is in the
Chattanooga rail yard just beyond the train shed. Lookout Mountain is in the distance. (*National Archives*)

Harpers Ferry was critical in many campaigns throughout the Eastern Theater. This 1858 view shows the Latrobian Truss—also referred to as a Bollman Truss—in its covered bridge stage, as it appeared when John Brown and his raiders tried to seize the arsenal and gun factory on October 16, 1859. The 900-foot span opened for service in 1837. Harpers Ferry would change hands 12 times during the war. (*Author's Collection*)

THREE

WHERE THE RIVERS MEET

"There stands Jackson like a stone wall! Rally behind the Virginians!"
—*Brigadier General Barnard E. Bee, CSA, at the First Battle of Manassas*

Situated at the confluence of the Potomac and Shenandoah rivers and with the Blue Ridge Mountains rising grandly from its sides, Harpers Ferry's rugged beauty was inescapable. Even restless Union occupiers in the throes of war could not ignore it. Colonel John White Geary would write, "The scenery around Harper's Ferry is majestically grand and such as bears an Almighty hand." Two man-made creations exalted the place in different ways that would, unfortunately, attract violence. These were the Baltimore & Ohio Railroad and the Chesapeake & Ohio Canal.

Harpers Ferry had long been home to an industrious community. The United States Arsenal and Armory were located there along with the valuable Hall's Rifle Works, a major firearms producer. John Brown's raid on the arsenal October 16, 1859, an event he hoped would spark a slave uprising, is considered one of the major catalysts of the war.

If war results from the breakdown of politics—leaving only violent reactions to injustices—then maybe the fuse of the Civil War had been lit even before John Brown's attempt to create insurrection. Bloody slave related confrontations had occurred in Kansas in the mid-1850s.

President Buchanan would find his America radicalized by John Brown's hostility, however. Such violence from the far end of the political spectrum inevitably prompts a violent response from the extreme opposite end.

Harpers Ferry would bear the brunt of much of this hostility. The story of Harpers Ferry does not receive as much attention in Civil War histories as it deserves. Brown's raid is recounted and the destruction of the bridge is mentioned, but the town was critical in numerous campaigns throughout the war. The Baltimore & Ohio Railroad was the Union's most important supply line, and part of the direct defense of Washington. The railroad's main stem narrowed to a chokehold through Harpers Ferry, making it the ideal target of repeated attacks.

Immediately after Virginia seceded in April 1861, the superintendent of the arsenal turned it and the garrison over to Virginia forces. In an act of sabotage to keep Confederates from seizing it, Lieutenant Roger Jones set fire to the arsenal buildings and then escaped into Pennsylvania.

Additional Confederate troops began arriving by April 27. They worked with existing regiments, picking and pawing through the ruins for salvageable tools and machines. What they gathered was sent on to Richmond.

Confederate General Joseph E. Johnston took over military operations at the town in May and was not long in realizing it could not be effectively defended. Union forces need only take up positions in the surrounding mountains. From those vantages they could use artillery to bombard the place into ruin. In June, he pulled out, moving his command to Winchester, Virginia.

In July, Union forces took control of the town only to be run out by Confederate cavalrymen under Captain Turner Ashby. The town would change hands four more times over the next six months.

The first year of the war had taken its toll on the picturesque town. The constant back and forth between occupiers left it ravaged— a once proud place left mirthless by all the fighting. Its inspiring beauty aside, Union General Nathaniel P. Banks found the wrecked town unremarkable when he arrived in late February 1862. He put down a strong foothold nonetheless, using it as a base for upcoming operations in the Shenandoah Valley.

These were but a few of the events that befell the citizens of Harpers Ferry. The town would ultimately change hands 12 times during the war. It was as if John Brown

had cursed it when his bloody raid failed. Anxiety over the town's identity would only deepen again when townsfolk found themselves no longer part of the Confederacy. On June 20, 1863 it became part of the newly formed Union state of West Virginia. Ironically, it was the first state to secede from the world's newest nation, the Confederate States of America.

The many artillery bombardments, sieges, fires, and natural floods left Harpers Ferry brooding and desolate. A visitor wrote in 1866, "The town itself lies in ruins . . . all about the town are rubbish, and filth and stench." The good people would strive to get it back to its former glory during post-war rebuilding.

Perhaps nothing was more dispiriting to the citizenry of Harper Ferry than the destruction of their pride of the valley, the massive covered railroad and turnpike bridge across the Potomac. Conceived in 1834 amidst bickering over using an existing 1824 toll bridge, the Baltimore & Ohio moved forward with plans of their own for a combination railroad and turnpike bridge. Construction of the $85,000 project began in 1835. Referred to as a Latrobian truss, the completed 900-foot span was an architectural triumph when opened for service in 1837. Vertical and diagonal iron cables, alternately providing tension and compression, braced the seven spans. Six piers were needed for support, five being in the river and the sixth resting on the C&O Canal towpath.

The railroad ran along the south side of the span. The turnpike took the north. A complex but beautiful modern span, it did have its problems, requiring foundational repairs, particularly to cracked support heads. The railroad made improvements at various times and in 1842 a junction switch was added about 265 feet out from the Harpers Ferry side for connection with the Winchester & Potomac Railroad. This created a new span with a rather tight curve to steer trains along the Potomac shoreline. The entire structure was eventually transformed into a covered bridge when carpenters sheathed it with boards and a tin roof. Apparently the clapboards were removed in warmer weather as some photos show it free of any siding. It must have been an ordeal for passengers traveling through the 900-foot covered bridge. Even with open vents it must have been dark and terribly smoky.

It was from within the darkness of the covered bridge that John Brown and his men fired shots at a train during his raid on October 16, 1859. An African-American porter at the Harpers Ferry station was shot and killed when he appeared at the bridge's opening to see what was going on. Local militia and angry citizens drove Brown and his men away from the bridge. The raiders holed themselves up in the town's firehouse, taking hostages with them. On October 18, General Robert E. Lee arrived by train with United States Marines. By then the vengeful citizens—many of them drunk—were pounding on the firehouse with hammers and whatever else they could get their hands on. Lee and his Marines quickly got the situation under control.

In April 1861, Confederate militia moved down the Orange & Alexandria and Manassas Gap Railroad, bound on capturing

Harpers Ferry. They held it until June when an overwhelming Union force approached, compelling the Confederates to abandon the town.

At 4 A.M. on June 14, 1861, Colonel Thomas J. (later "Stonewall") Jackson's men blew up the splendid B&O bridge. The explosions—a series of nerve-shattering blasts that shook the earth and echoed off the mountains—jolted the townsfolk from their sleep. It was something they would have to get used to however. The bridge would be rebuilt and destroyed nine times during the war.

The Baltimore & Ohio Railroad Company, established in 1827, was one of America's first common carriers. From the beginning it built substantial masonry bridges, culverts, and buildings. This may have come from not knowing the exact tolerances and strengths that were needed to support their new railroad. It was all so new that it would be better to over-build than risk disaster. Whatever the reasoning, much of what they built is still with us and some constructions are still used.

At the start of the war, the B&O line stretched from its eastern headquarters in Baltimore to Wheeling, Virginia, and the Ohio River in the west. Its roster included 128 passenger cars, 3,451 freight cars, 236 fine locomotives, and 513 miles of track running in states south of the Mason-Dixon Line. It was presided over by an amazingly capable and patriotic president, John H. Garrett, who would hold the position until his death in 1884. Garrett skillfully negotiated his railroad through the impact of over 140 direct attacks during the Civil War.

Jackson's assaults on the B&O in 1861 gave birth to what some consider a remarkable railroad fable. It lingers so deeply in the lore of the Civil War that it cannot go without mention. The "Great Train Raid of 1861," commencing with the June 14, 1861, demolition of the Harpers Ferry bridge, triggered a Confederate rampage against the B&O. Additionally, it hampered traffic on the critical C&O Canal and disrupted vital Federal telegraph communications between Washington, DC, Baltimore, and the interior of the nation.

The Federal government had been using the B&O's double tracked mainline to transport tons of coal mined in the subterranean coal-rich Ohio Valley. It was destined for northern industries and Union naval bases in Baltimore. From wharves in Baltimore the coal went to navy warships setting off to blockade harbors in the Deep South. Other trains transported tons of flour, livestock, and produce.

According to the story, Colonel Jackson devised a plan to attract and then bottle-up these trains—which he had been allowing to run to appease frustrated Marylanders. He restricted trains to only two hour's passage through Harpers Ferry. Trains soon became backed-up on both sides of the river. On May 23, 1861, Jackson's operatives cut off train movements completely. Trains backed up in the double track blocks south of Harpers Ferry were now trapped as far back as the large rail yard at Martinsburg. This daring operation constituted the largest capture of engines and rolling stock of the war.

Jackson now had to find a way to get as much of this equipment, isolated on 76-miles of combined B&O and Winchester &

Potomac trackage out of the area and into Confederate hands. The W&P spur off the B&O at Harpers Ferry was the best route even though it used inferior flat rail track. What followed were as series adventures in which dozens of bridges were destroyed, miles of track wrecked and locomotives and rolling stock burned, disabled, or pushed off bridges. The most fantastic aspect of all this was the claim that between 14 and 19 engines were pulled from Martinsburg to Strasburg, Virginia, on hastily built wagons and dollies drawn by 40 horse teams. There *are* eyewitness accounts of a few locomotives being hauled through the streets on wagons. One was a smaller old style "Dutch Wagon" class from the 1840s and the other a Camel—a bulky coal-burning brute favored by the B&O. There may even have been a second Camel. According to the story, the locomotives were dismantled, placed on wagons and dragged first along the Martinsburg and Winchester Turnpike and then up the Valley Turnpike to Strasburg. During reassembly by Rebel railroad corps, the cursing started. It turned out the engines were of a different gauge than the Manassas Gap tracks they were intended to run on. Being useless for service in the Shenandoah Valley, they were once again dismantled and sent piecemeal to Richmond. However, there is little official documentation to suggest anything of this magnitude ever happened, despite the persistent stories.

We are left with a dilemma because the Great Train Raid of 1861 appears in countless histories of the war. The tale was drawn from the writings of John D. Imboden, who was involved in several raids on the B&O. He recorded his recollections when of advanced years in *Harper's Magazine*. In his biography of Stonewall Jackson, historian James I. Robertson puts forth that Imboden invented the tale. Robertson's scrutiny of existing documentation surrounding the raid led him to the following conclusion:

> Delightful as the story is, it is totally fictional. Jackson could not have committed these actions on his own, and he had no orders to disrupt the B&O completely. The Confederate government would not have issued such a directive while making overtures of cooperation with Maryland. If such destruction had occurred, the Union government would have screamed in protest and initiated retribution. No such reactions are recorded.

Jackson had been given strict orders from Robert E. Lee not to disrupt B&O operations. Lee told him to limit activities to purely defensive measures. President Jefferson Davis wanted to present the Confederacy positively to Maryland, offering inducements to join his new nation. Among his gestures was leaving Maryland out of his declaration of war against the North. Disruption of commerce on the scale Jackson's raids would have drawn Marylanders' wrath.

Notwithstanding this, Jackson unquestionably went on an orgy of destruction against the B&O after blowing up the Harpers Ferry Bridge. Many bridges in the vicinity were demolished. At least 36 miles of track were torn up and over 100 miles of telegraph lines were pulled down. Perhaps 42 locomotives were destroyed along with many pieces of rolling stock. Confederates fell on the locomotives parked in the vicinity of Martinsburg and its large rail yard with ham-

mers, crowbars—anything that would inflict damage. Drive rods were bent. Gauges were smashed. Throttles were twisted. Fittings and pipes were sawn, punctured, or pried apart. In some instances water was drained from engines and fires started in the firebox. The heat distorted flues and warped the fire pan. All other rolling stock was torched.

Jackson regretted having wrecked equipment that would have been of great service to the Confederacy. A man of tender letters to his beloved wife Anna, he wrote her his regrets, "It was sad work but I had my orders and my duty was to obey."

But certainly Jackson's operations against the railroad were destructive enough to stop service between Wheeling and Baltimore for ten months. Financial losses were estimated at $700,000. Fourteen engines were, by hook or by crook, captured and sent deeper into the land of cotton. Twelve engines, eleven tenders and the boiler of a thirteenth engine would be returned after the war. This was confirmed by a ranking B&O official who complained that everything was in terrible shape. It was still valuable though and what wasn't repairable was incorporated into other equipment.

President Garrett summed it up in his Annual Report of the B&O for 1861. He wrote:

> On May 28, 1861, general possession was taken by the Confederate forces of more than one hundred miles of the Main Stem, embroiling chiefly the region between Point of Rocks and Cumberland. Occasional movements were also made, accompanied by considerable destruction up the roads between Cumberland and Wheeling, and

Grafton and Parkersburg, during the fiscal year. The Protection of the Government was not restored throughout the line until March 1862, when the reconstruction was pressed with great energy, and the line reopened on the 29th of that month.

Garrett was disgusted by the Federal government's lack of protection for his railroad particularly when the government relied upon it so heavily. The indifference continued throughout the war as the railroad endured continued attacks by raiders. Even the defense of Washington, DC, was imperiled by this reckless lack of strategy. It allowed continued Confederate assaults in the area—much of it against the B&O.

The capital would have a harrowingly close call during the Battle of Monocacy on July 9, 1864. Garrett's railroad agents observed Confederate movements in and around the Monocacy Station district. Garrett passed intelligence detailing troop movements and intentions to the War Department 11 days prior to the battle.

Confederate troops under Lt. Gen. Jubal A. Early marched through the Shenandoah Valley from Lynchburg deliberately skirting the Union garrison at Harpers Ferry. They crossed the Potomac River at Shepherdstown and entered Maryland on July 5-6. During this time, Union forces were moved along the B&O. Lincoln would twice contact Garrett directly for updated information.

A hastily assembled Union force under Maj. Gen. Lew Wallace attempted to push back Early's invading forces along the Monocacy River during the following week. Other Federal reinforcements from Ricketts's Division of the VI Corps were rushed in to assist but with no success. Wallace was outflanked and defeated.

When General Ulysses S. Grant learned Confederate forces under Early had entered Maryland, near panic set in. He quickly put the remainder of VI Corps on transports at City Point and rushed them to Washington. Although Union forces under Wallace had been defeated, the battle gave Grant enough time to get VI Corps moving. On July 11, Confederate troops under Early stood, unbelievably, at the outskirts of Washington. The VI Corps began arriving that night and were quickly incorporated into the capital's defenses. Early's troops were finally turned back in what later was called the "Battle that Saved Washington."

The B&O's contributions in this important action compelled President Lincoln to praise Garrett as:

> The right arm of the Federal Government in the aid he rendered the authorities in preventing the Confederates from seizing Washington and securing its retention as the Capital of the Loyal States.

This praise may have provided minimal satisfaction to Garrett who saw his railroad subjected to continued merciless pounding. The cash compensation from Washington may have offset some of this, but the matter of sufficient Federal protection remained contentious. Blockhouses were built to protect major bridges. Although manned occasionally by Federal troops, bridges still came down at an alarming rate.

As critical as the railroad was in protecting the capital, a lack of sympathy persisted. It is evident in Union General Philip Sheridan's curt refusal to a request for help: "There is no interest suffering here except the Baltimore and Ohio and I will not divide my forces to protect it."

❧

Affectionately known as "Stonewall," "Tom Fool," "Old Jack," and "Old Blue Light," Thomas Jonathan Jackson was one of the most brilliant tactical commanders in United States history. Lee need only tell him what his objective was and Stonewall would employ innovative and audacious tactics to get it done, often in the face of insurmountable odds. Jackson's initial assaults on the B&O were just some of the accomplishments that vaulted him to second most revered Southern general behind Robert E. Lee. He was not done with the railroad, by a long shot.

Events were set in motion during the Shenandoah Valley Campaign of 1862. On May 30, Jackson attacked Harpers Ferry but was driven off by Union general Rufus Saxton.

Another attack on the town would come three months later as General Lee launched his invasion of the North. The output of the restored arsenal and firearms manufactory were much desired but Lee's primary goal was the B&O to sustain his supply lines from the Shenandoah Valley. In the event of failure, he would need the railroad for his retreat behind the Blue Ridge mountains. As a precaution, he had already blown up the B&O's iron bridge at Monocacy in his September invasion of Maryland, an act intended to keep the Yankees off his trail.

Lee, in a dangerous maneuver that ulti-mately brought America its deadliest day, divided his army of approximately 40,000 into four sections. Using the cover of the mountains, he sent three divisions under Jackson to capture Harpers Ferry.

Fighting in the Battle of Harpers Ferry started September 13 with the capture of Maryland Heights and Loudon Heights. The Confederates commenced a punishing bombardment on September 14 causing the Federal garrison to surrender on Bolivar Heights just west of town the next day. The surrender of 15,000 U.S. troops would not be equaled until World War II.

This action, though a victory, created an unexpected delay, forcing Lee to regroup at Sharpsburg, Maryland, a mere eight miles north of the B&O's Kearneysville station. Two days later, on September 16, Lee's Army of Northern Virginia was confronted by Maj. Gen. George B. McClellan's Union forces.

The Maryland countryside was illuminated in autumnal glory. The populace of Sharpsburg, unsettled by war, at least hoped to enjoy the pastoral beauty of the season; its colored trees tilting over Antietam Creek and acres of withered cornstalks stirring in soft Maryland breezes. In the midst of relishing the bounty of their harvest, Lee blundered into town with his Army of Northern Virginia. The war had come to their backyard.

In the soft dawn glow of September 16, 1862, Hooker's corps launched a powerful attack on Lee's left flank. At Miller's cornfield an ebb and flow of attack and counterattack commenced. The tranquil reverence of Dunker Church was enveloped in savage warfare. Heaps of bodies began to fill the Sunken Road.

Young men who had previously fired a gun only when hunting now charged with bayonet-tipped muskets across fields. Had love of Lee and the Cause filled the Rebel soul with such controlling hatred? To what level did the Yankee desire to keep the nation together, even though many thought slaves inferior, fill them with vengeful savagery? War, in its ugly way, had taken control of them, turning both sides dark and murderous.

On that day decent young men let go of their dreams of pretty women, of happy homes and barn dances, to trample across fields while artillery shells exploded around them. Arms and legs of fellow soldiers or maybe even brothers hurled sickeningly past them, whisking blood and gore across their faces. All of it was made even more unreal by the threatening Rebel war cry combining with the forceful Yankee holler.

Lee was outnumbered two-to-one but threw his entire army against McClellan who foolishly did not use his entire force to counter. This enabled Lee to fight the battle to a standstill. Loyal Stonewall hurried his forces into action and went right to work.

That night the battered armies regrouped. Lee had suffered crippling casualties but would continue to skirmish the next day even as he removed his wounded soldiers south. At nightfall he ordered his bloodied army to withdraw across the Potomac where it limped deeper into the Shenandoah Valley. The battle, though a Union strategic victory, was nonetheless indecisive. Casualties were estimated at 23,100.

Had McClellan pursued, he very well could have destroyed Lee's army and hastened an end to the War of the Rebellion. It was exactly this kind of thing that added age

wrinkles to Lincoln's face: uncertainty, timidity, and hesitancy amongst his generals. Lincoln had been through this with General Pope who delivered a humiliating defeat at the Second Battle of Bull Run and again with General Burnside after his costly loss at Fredericksburg in December 1862.

Lee certainly reacted to the North's incompetent generals. But even as early as Fredericksburg his soul seemed poisoned by the carnage. "It is well that war is so terrible—we should grow too fond of it," he would say. Maybe he had ridden too long at the head of wagon trains filled with wounded that stretched for miles.

On September 22, 1862, five days after Antietam, President Lincoln issued his preliminary Emancipation Proclamation freeing slaves in America. A second part to the proclamation would follow and it made clear the end of slavery had become the primary objective of this war.

Lee's retreat into the Shenandoah Valley left Harpers Ferry indefensible. Stonewall Jackson withdrew from the town, blowing up the arsenal as he left. This second destruction of the arsenal and firearm manufactory would end a tradition of firearms production dating back to 1799. A week later Harpers Ferry was back in Union hands.

Stonewall wouldn't stay away for long. In October he was back in the region, returning to Martinsburg where he renewed his attacks on the B&O. This time his thoughts were nothing less than total obliteration. He destroyed 20 miles of track and bridges between Harpers Ferry and North Mountain. Determined to not leave anything behind the Federals could use, he destroyed the roundhouse and turntable at

Martinsburg along with shops, wood ricks, water towers, rolling stock, and storage sheds. Afterwards, B&O repairmen and Federal Construction Corps patiently went about repairing everything. The Confederate general had certainly kept not only the B&O but also other railroads busy cleaning up messes he left in his wake.

In the first week of May 1863, Lee decisively defeated the Union Army under General Hooker at Chancellorsville. Again Stonewall directed his corps on a bold flanking maneuver to the right of the Union lines. It would turn out to be one of the most brilliant movements of the war.

The fighting ended May 2, when darkness set in. Stonewall and his staff were returning to camp when they were mistakenly fired upon by a Confederate North Carolina regiment. Several of the men were killed. Jackson was shot twice in the left arm and once in the right hand. A sudden volley of incoming artillery rounds prevented Stonewall from getting immediate help. When he was finally lifted onto a stretcher, he was dropped because of the chaos caused by the exploding shells. His left arm was amputated and he was taken to Fairfield plantation to recover. Pneumonia set in and Stonewall died on May 10. Always a deeply spiritual man, he managed to utter from his deathbed, "It's the Lord's Day; my wish is fulfilled. I have always desired to die on Sunday."

Lee was devastated. "I have lost my right arm," he lamented. It would be a huge blow to the Southern Cause. It is more than probable Lee would have prevailed at Gettysburg if he had Stonewall there with him.

Stonewall's operations against the B&O in the first two years of the war were effective,

Handcars were a good way to check a railroad for damage. (*Library of Congress*)

but they would be overcome. It is more than likely that when news of Stonewall's death reached the railroad's leadership that not a single tear was shed, except perhaps in rapturous joy.

A partial list of raids and actions against the Baltimore & Ohio Railroad is daunting:

The Great Train Raid, May 1861.
Martinsburg Train Raid, June 1861.
Leesburg Train Raid, August 1861.
Romney Expedition, January 1862.
Raids by Brigadier General A.G. Jenkins in the fall of 1862.
Jones-Imboden Raid, April–May 1863.
Battle of Monocacy, July 1864.
Turner Ashby Raids with his "Black Horse" cavalry.

In addition, there were numerous attacks on the railroad in towns and cities it served. Among them were, of course, Harpers Ferry, Opequon, Winchester, and Cumberland.

Not all the destruction along the B&O was at the hands of Johnny Reb. The Yankees had to inflict damage at times to thwart enemy advances. On July 5, 1863, Federal troops got their chance to destroy the flimsy replacement trestle bridge at Harpers Ferry to thwart possible Confederate movements.

Such was persistence of enemy attacks on the B&O during the war that railroad officials were lucky if they could claim ownership of the entire line for more than six months at a time. In spite of this, the railroad prospered. Federal compensation, increased freight and, surprisingly, an up-tick in passenger service kept the company in the black.

Repairs and rebuilding aside, the well-managed company would net four and a half million dollars profit in 1863. On the important Laurel–Washington route, work began on replacing old style light U-rail mounted on stringers with heavy 60-pound T-rail spiked to white oak crossties. Former wooden bridges along one third of the important Washington Branch were being replaced with iron to accommodate the double tracking of the route in 1864. With continued war needs in their thoughts, B&O management set to rebuilding nearly 200 cars and constructing 263 new ones at their Mount Clare shops, the latter possibly with an eye towards postwar prosperity.

Assaults on the railroad during 1864 lessened, but on July 2, when Confederates reached the gates of Washington, the railroad sent an ironclad train to drive off an attack by Jubal A. Early at Great Cacapon River during the Battle of Monocacy.

As trains went in to get the wounded from the battle, Early began drifting past the B&O. He stopped to harass workers installing the second row of tracks on the Washington Branch but then turned his sights on crippling the Philadelphia, Wilmington, & Baltimore Railroad and other regional lines.

The Baltimore & Ohio Railroad would thrive in spite of the beating it took. Other lines would do well, both North and South, but some railroads would never recover from the toll the war took on them.

This 1861 view of Harpers Ferry shows the spur added in 1842 to the Latrobian Truss bridge to connect with the Winchester & Potomac Railroad. Six piers were used to support the five spans. Five were in the river and the sixth rested on the Chesapeake and Ohio Canal towpath. The empty canal is visible at the bottom of the photo. (*Library of Congress*)

A combination of masonry piers and wood trestles supported the Harpers Ferry side of the bridge. The bridge guardhouse is visible in the center of the image. (*Library of Congress*)

On June 14, 1861, at 4 A.M., the bridge collapsed into the river after a series of explosions ordered by Confederate Col. Thomas J. Jackson, who would soon earn the sobriquet, "Stonewall." It was something the townsfolk would have to get used to. The bridge would be rebuilt and destroyed nine times during the war. The two small patches of land in the river right of the bridge were remnants of footings for the original 1824 toll bridge. (*Library of Congress*)

Techniques for destroying rail continue in northern Virginia. They would be put to the test sooner rather than later. Tall levers are linked together and fastened to the track. When the levels were forced up, the rail would be twisted into a corkscrew, rendering it useless. (*Library of Congress*)

The Mason-built *Genl. Haupt* glistens in the Virginia sun. (*National Archives*)

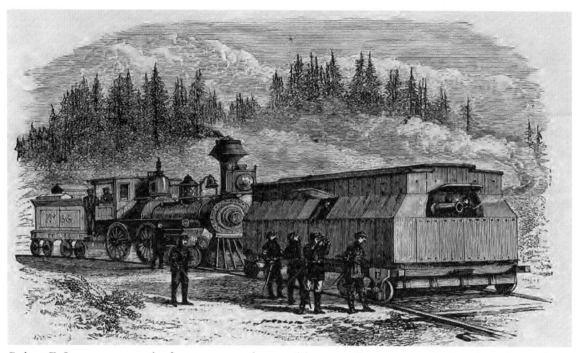

Robert E. Lee was among the first to contemplate a rail-borne artillery car. A rendering of an advanced armored car utilizing iron plating was based on eyewitness accounts. (*Author's Collection*)

Andrew J. Russell photographed the first train over the new bridge at Bull Run in the spring of 1863. The photo holds an interesting detail shown in the image below. Russell's photograph captured what may be the only existing image of an armored train car in the Civil War. The gun port is opened, exposing the cannon. It was built on a flat car and the preceding car was part of the unit, perhaps carrying the ammunition. (*Library of Congress*)

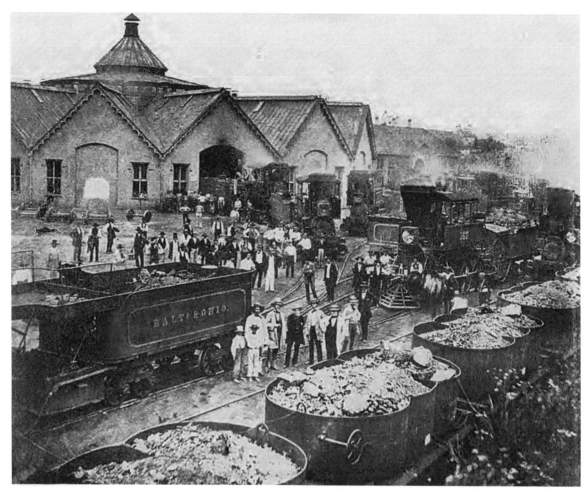

The original Baltimore & Ohio roundhouse at Martinsburg, Virginia, was destroyed during the war. This roundhouse was built at the end of the war and is identical to the one destroyed. The railroad had a fondness for coal-burning Camel-back locomotives. In the foreground are round pot cars used for hauling iron and coal. (*Author's Collection*)

Federal forces are protecting the magnificent B&O Thomas Viaduct over the Patapsco River between Relay and Elkridge Landing, Maryland. Built 1833-1835, it was the first multi-span masonry bridge in the country and the first built on a curving alignment. The B&O was the Union's most important supply line into Washington. In 1861, Stonewall Jackson attacked the railroad relentlessly. Fortunately this bridge survived. (*Author's Collection*)

Soldiers at the famous Relay House on the B&O Washington Branch are there to inspect all westbound trains for Rebel soldiers and supplies trying to reach Harpers Ferry. B&O passengers had to be relayed here by buggy and stagecoach to board trains. (*Author's Collection*)

Railroad men point to damage inflicted on the *Fred Leach* while in service on the Orange & Alexandria line near Union Mills, Virginia. Shells pierced the smoke stack and the tender flange. There is also damage to its domes, boiler, and drive rods. (*National Archives*)

One of Stonewall Jackson's boldest actions against the B&O was heralded as The Great Train Raid of 1861. Part fact, part fable, at least two captured locomotives were dismantled and moved on wagons down the turnpike from Martinsburg to Strasburg, Virginia. One was a "Dutch Wagon." This 1854 Norris built 4-4-0 is an example. It was an internal drive locomotive with the cylinders and drive mechanism hidden under the boiler and between the drivers. (*Author's Collection*)

Confederates blew up the beautiful Baltimore & Ohio spans over the Monongahela at Fairmont, Virginia. It is pictured here in the 1850s. (*Library of Congress*)

Undaunted, the B&O replaced the Fairmont spans with nearly identical ones. They used the revolutionary Bollman Truss almost exclusively. They were fabricated entirely of iron. The new bridge is pictured here in 1865. (*Library of Congress*)

Bales of hay shipped in from northern farms are being loaded on flatcars at City Point. They would be sent to feed the thousands of horses used by Grant's Army. (*Library of Congress*)

A birds-eye view taken from the dome of the O&A roundhouse at Alexandria shows the east yards and the expansion of machine and repair shops. (*Library of Congress*)

Confederate raiders have left a trail of destruction on the O&A at Catlett's Station. Construction Corps workers are assessing the damage. Debris scattered along both sides of the track suggest a lot of rolling stock was destroyed. The O&A took the hardest beatings in the vicinity of Culpeper, Fairfax, Manassas Junction, Brandy Station, and along the Warrenton Branch. (*Library of Congress*)

On August 9, 1864, two Confederate secret agents smuggled a time bomb aboard a barge at City Point that was loaded with ammunition. When the bomb exploded, it vaporized the barge and destroyed another. Buildings and equipment along the wharf were destroyed or damaged. At least 43 men were killed and many more wounded. The explosion was felt ten miles away. (*Library of Congress*)

Railroad activities go on in the distance at Fairfax Station on the O&A. These fellows stand in a desolated landscape. The countryside up to the far ridge has been stripped of trees. This was often the case wherever railroads brought armies. What wasn't processed into fortifications and buildings was fed into locomotives and campfires. (*National Archives*)

The *Genl. Haupt* is pulling a train used in excavations for auxiliary trackage, including a wye, on the O&A in the vicinity of Devereux Station. Mr. Haupt is the dark clad bearded fellow standing at the center on the embankment. (*National Archives*)

The sleek Mason-built *Genl. Haupt* has since been renamed the *Genl. J. C. Robinson* in this photo at City Point. Beyond the locomotives are twin water tanks. (*Library of Congress*)

Soldiers cool off in the North Anna River, Virginia, in May 1864. In the distance are the ruins of a Richmond & Fredericksburg Railroad bridge. (*National Archives*)

Clerks of the Commissary Depot pose next to crates of supplies at Aquia Creek Landing, Virginia. (*Library of Congress*)

Workers with the Construction Corps complete the final stages of the new truss over Bull Run in 1863. The trusses and some sub-assemblies were built in the lumberyard at Alexandria, Virginia. (*Library of Congress*)

Federal pickets guard two trains coming into Union Mills Station on the O&A. Twin water tanks slated the endless thirst of locomotives. A fresh supply of wheels is headed to the shops. An idea of how backbreaking railroad construction could be is in the large fill the distant trains are riding on. All that was done with shovels and wheelbarrows. (*Library of Congress*)

A member of the U.S. Colored Troops stands guard at the head of impressive 12-pounder bronze howitzers at City Point. The "Napoleon" gun was the workhorse of artillery units. (*Library of Congress*)

The Construction Corps had its hands full dealing with raider destruction at Manassas Station in August 1862. Methods of derailment included mines placed under track, removing spikes and leaving the rail in place, and something as simple as hooking a horseshoe over a rail. (*Author's Collection*)

The rail facilities at Aquia Creek included an enlistment headquarters for men brought in by train. Here recently arrived African Americans wait their turn to enlist as the headquarters housed in the Provost Marshal office. (*Library of Congress*)

The covered Danville Railroad bridge connected Richmond, Virginia, with Belle Island in the James River. Among the factories on Belle Island was the important Old Dominion Iron and Nail Works shown beyond the small flat cars and iron pot cars in the enlargement below. (*National Archives*)

Two guarded USMRR trains are stopped on O&A tracks near Union Mills, Virginia. Wooded areas were dangerous because they gave cover to raiding parties. (*Library of Congress*)

Union soldiers endure a hot dusty Virginia day at Catlett's Station. The station was the site of numerous engagements throughout the war. (*Library of Congress*)

The three-story Hanover Junction Station with its battlement style roof, first story veranda, and ticket window was built 1852. It housed hotel rooms, railroad offices, a telegraph station, and living quarters for the stationmaster and his family—a common practice at rural stations. Confederate cavalry held the junction June 27, 1863, destroying bridges, track, and some buildings but sparing the station. Union wounded from the Battle of Gettysburg passed through the junction while being taken to hospitals in York, Harrisburg, and Baltimore. Lincoln arrived here on the Northern Central Railway from Baltimore and then changed trains to Gettysburg. (*Library of Congress*)

At approximately 4 P.M. Wednesday, November 18, 1863, a photographer on the roof of a boxcar took this photograph of dignitaries at Hanover Junction, Pennsylvania. They were en route to Gettysburg to hear Lincoln's dedication of the cemetery. The track on the left is the Hanover Branch Railroad. Veering right is the Northern Central Railway. The engine has an old style strap iron pilot but a cap-smoke stack more typical of modern coal burners. (*Library of Congress*)

Events at Gettysburg raised alerts at railroads in Pennsylvania. That included the Philadelphia & Reading Railroad. The sign along the massive train shed at Harrisburg, pictured in 1863, reads: "Philadelphia & Reading Rail Road. Cars to Philadelphia, Reading, Pottsville, Lebanon, Allentown, Raston & New York." (*Author's Collection*)

The impressive Meadville, Pennsylvania, station in a photo dated 1865 serviced the broad gauge Atlantic & Great Western, later the Erie, Railroad. The unusual twin station connected by an over track shed had a 100-room hotel and dining room "as long as a train." (*Author's Collection*)

A Union camp occupies the area near the Culpeper Court House, Virginia, rail facilities. The tranquil wheat fields, for which Culpeper County was noted, endured the rumble of trains headed to the battles of Cedar Mountain, Second Manassas, the Maryland Campaign, Antietam, Fredericksburg, Gettysburg, Brandy Station, Rappahannock Station, and Grant's Overland Campaign. Note the trains in the left background; see page 159. (*Library of Congress*)

FOUR

RAILROADS IN THE LAND OF JUBILEE

"Without firing a gun, without drawing a sword, should they [Northerners] make war upon us [Southerners], we could bring the whole world to our feet. What would happen if no cotton was furnished for three years? . . . England would topple head-long and carry the whole civilized world with her. No, you dare not make war on cotton! No power on earth dares make war upon it. Cotton is King."
—*Senator James Hammond of South Carolina in 1858*

There is a popular perception that Southern railroads prior to the Civil War were universally inferior if not wholly decrepit in comparison with those in the North. We can imagine sweaty sluggish old engines chugging through the low country, along moss-draped forests, to ports with boxcars of processed cotton lint from mills. The cotton would be transferred to steamers and sailing vessels bound for Europe or New England's textile mills.

Maybe Southern railroads were not always as fine as their Yankee counterparts, but the North had its share of near bankrupt, ill-conceived, dirty lines. Many fell in and out of receivership or were overtaken by better-run companies. When the war broke out, the South had more running track miles than England, an impressive statistic were it not that the North had twice that.

Many southern railroads were planned with hopeful prospects extending beyond hauling cotton and tobacco from Delta plantations. Although Southern social and political life revolved around King Cotton, they seem almost ashamed of their healthy industrial base. Not every Southerner approved of slavery. Most Rebels who fell in battle never believed they'd own slaves. The enduring image of large plantations worked by slaves should be weighed with the reality that there were many more smaller cotton farms worked by whites.

The forward-looking plans of more prestigious southern railroads certainly anticipated industrial growth and increased access to northern markets. There was lumber aplenty to be hauled, and coal; goods from foundries, passenger service, manufactured goods, livestock, and a hundred other commodities.

It was a frustrating thing for railroad companies, who, together with factory owners, ran into an unspoken aversion from southern leaders to industrial development. Ironically they would encounter the same attitude from Confederate leaders during the war—even after suffering from the scarcity of necessary materials due to a restrained manufacturing base.

These railroad owners must have shook their heads in dismay at aristocrats so lost in the past, so blind to their dream world being wrecked, that even the bursting of cannon shells could not knock such fantasies from their minds. What if the Confederacy did win? Did they think they could survive without growing their manufacturing base? Certainly the North would turn a cold shoulder to them, at least for a generation or two before the lure of commerce returned them to more sensible policies.

Even before the war, as the possibility of secession took hold across the South, it was approached with a wishful naivete. Secessionists figured that if they simply told the North they wanted to be left alone, to drift towards their own ideas of nationhood, everything would work out for the better. Of course the North glared icily at such nonsense. When war broke out William T. Sherman expressed these thoughts in a letter to Southern friend:

> You people of the South don't know what you are doing. This country will be drenched in blood, and God only knows how it will end. It is all folly, madness, a crime against civilization! You people speak so lightly of war; you don't know what you're talking about. War is a terrible thing. You mistake, too, the people of the North. They are a

peaceable people but an earnest people, and they will fight, too. They are not going to let this country be destroyed without a mighty effort to save it.

> Besides, where are your men and appliances of war to contend against them? The North can make a steam engine, locomotive, or railway car; hardly a yard of cloth or pair of shoes can you make. You are rushing into war with one of the most powerful, ingeniously mechanical, and determined people on Earth—right at your doors.

> You are bound to fail. Only in your spirit and determination are you prepared for war. In all else you are totally unprepared, with a bad case to start with. At first you will make headway, but as your limited resources begin to fail, shut out from the markets of Europe as you will be, your cause will begin to wane. If your people will but stop and think, they must see in the end that you will surely fail.

So we are left with baffling ironies. The South had a healthy manufacturing base capable of sustaining a smaller war. When it found itself embroiled in a prolonged conflict, it foolishly rejected sensible mobilization policies that would have generated tremendous wartime growth. Instead they were left scrambling for supplies while ignoring the sound advice of their own industrialists. Their own constitution stipulated, "No encouragement to domestic industry." Such a course—had they won—may have doomed them to poverty.

In 1861, the South had at least ten rolling mills for producing and fabricating iron. Certainly adequate for peace time production but without access to new machinery and replacement parts, their ability to re-roll war damaged rail and fabricate replacement parts was limited. And to make matters worse, they sometimes had to destroy a rolling mill to keep it out of Union hands. The Markham & Schofield rolling mill, for example, situated beside the Georgia Railroad tracks outside Atlanta, was destroyed by retreating Confederates along with two trains totaling 81 cars loaded with ammunition and supplies. It was during this action that the famous locomotive *General* was damaged.

The rivalry between some aristocratic planters and southern manufacturers was long-standing and terse. This may have had something to do with many of the manufacturers originally having come from the North. Allegiance to the Confederacy or the United States aside, they were unashamedly motivated by profits. It was their business sense that got the Confederate government to enact tariffs in 1861—as the North had—to help finance the war.

The blockade of Southern ports under the Union's Anaconda Plan severely reduced access of much needed materials for railroads and factories. Yankee smugglers, in cahoots with Rebel agents, got some supplies through. Again, profit overshadowed allegiance. The increased reliance on trains to move precious materials between factories added to the wear and tear the lines were already suffering from wartime transport of armies and weapons. Part of the Federal strategy was to smash the South's industrial capacity. They would do this by going after their railroads.

Railroads servicing the South and border states were subject to military attacks but northern lines would have their problems as well. Their equipment and rolling stock was

Originally misidentified as the *Hero*, this is actually the famous *General*. It is shown after taking a merciless beating during the evacuation of Atlanta. (*Author's Collection*)

run ragged by the increased wartime traffic. The transport of soldiers, coal, wood, horses, cannon, livestock, and a thousand other needs ground down rails, ties, and rolling stock. Government compensation for wartime transport was often generous but a lot of money had to go back into maintenance.

Iron rail predominated in both the North and the South although some steel was being introduced. Steel was far superior but expensive. (The Pennsylvania Railroad experimented with steel topped rails to slow down deterioration.) Even under normal use, iron rail required constant maintenance. It tended to laminate—or flake off the top—weakening the rail so that it could fracture under the weight of a locomotive. The worn down spot, if not addressed, could cause flat spots on wheels. This could rattle a freight car to pieces. With replacement rail nearly impossible to locate, Confederate crews would be sent out to cut the damaged section out and weld the two remaining pieces together.

Scarcity of nearly everything railroad-related left most Southern railroads perpetually needful. Many of their lines were intended for seasonal use, transporting produce, fertilizer, and farm products between plantations and coastal wharves. In most cases they required limited rolling stock, usually just box and flat cars. The need to transport freight to another railroad was not as common in the operations of most companies as in the North.

Locomotives and rolling stock on many of their short lines were in questionable condition before the war. With added wartime use, equipment was pushed dangerously beyond acceptable tolerances. Engine freeze-ups, broken axles, overheated journals, rupturing chassis, and weakened bridges filled engineers with dread. Running trains over irregular track could cause rail ends to cup or twist up. Another danger was rail spreading from weakened ties or vibration.

The South produced less than 10 percent of their own engines, preferring the well-crafted machines turned out by elite northern manufacturers. Even the names of these builders had the ring of prestige: Mason Machine Works, Amoskeag, Danforth, Cooke & Company, William Swinburne, and Manchester Locomotive Works.

A handful of Southern builders, with equally impressive names, turned out limited machines. One was the noted Tredegar Iron Works in Richmond. It rolled 70 locomotives from its erecting shops between 1850 and 1860. Uriah Wells—sometimes called

the Appomattox Locomotive Works—produced around 20 machines in its Petersburg, Virginia, shops during the 1850s. Covington Locomotive Works of Covington, Kentucky, produced a few locomotives in the 1850s. Kentucky Locomotive Works made a handful of engines in its Louisville shops. Smith and Perkins, a builder in Alexandria, rolled out about 50 locomotives in the 1850s.

In 1862 Confederate railroads could be expected to carry a large variety of goods. Here is but a brief sampling: Licorice, anvils, undressed marble, mill stones, beets, oysters and clams (in shell), plaster, fire engines, cigars, saddlery, snuff, feathers, Epsom salts, fire crackers, corks, soap (fancy and common), plaster, beer, stoves, lightning rods, mattresses, beeswax, bath tubs, turpentine, billiard tables, carriages, and hair—probably horse hair for stuffing furniture.

The number of events that required the use of railroads in the Civil War, from tasks as important as moving thousands of troops to the mundane transport of mustache wax and spur rivets, run in the thousands and are therefore too numerous to chronicle here. A look at the activities of some Southern lines, both large and small, is certainly worthwhile. Nearly every line that has made it into some form of historical record is usually accompanied with the generic, "This railroad was critical in the Civil War." It is probably safe to say that any railroad, North or South, that could run a train from one place to another was critical, such was the demand to move things.

Most Southerners had limited affection for their railroad tradition, a system that generally met their needs. The Wilmington & Weldon Railroad in North Carolina was once the longest in the world at 161 1/2 miles when completed in 1840. Originally named the Wilmington & Raleigh Railroad, it ran between the state's largest port city at Wilmington in New Hanover County to Weldon in Halifax County. In 1855, it was renamed the Wilmington & Weldon. Its founders wanted to capitalize on the industry and agriculture of the Roanoke River valley. In time it emerged as a major rail hub in eastern North Carolina with an eye keenly trained to exploit commerce to the north.

During the war it was exalted as the "Lifeline of the Confederacy," moving much needed supplies from the single open Confederate port at Wilmington to Lee's army in Virginia and elsewhere in the Confederacy. Successful blockade-runners brought valuable replacement parts to the port at Wilmington to be distributed to Confederate roads that would include the W&W. These items included steam gauges, boilerplate, tires, belting, rail, and even basics such as tin, oil, paint, spikes, and screws.

Union troops eventually captured Wilmington and took full control of the railroad, effectively cutting off this important supply line. The loss of Wilmington figured heavily in forcing Lee's surrender at Appomattox.

The New Orleans, Opelousas & Great Western Railroad had 83 miles of T-rail track across which it would run, variously, 12 locomotives and nearly 230 cars. It had 16 stations and enjoyed a robust passenger business, bringing folks to waiting steamers at Brashear, Louisiana, twice a week. War careened onto its rails almost immediately. The Union blockade of Southern ports led

to a desperate effort by state and railroad officials to extend the line to Orange, Texas. Perhaps they could coax ways to secure railroad supplies from western lines. With hopes of keeping supplies flowing into the Confederacy, they came close to accomplishing their goal of running 45 miles of track from Brashear to New Iberia, Louisiana.

In May 1862, Union troops captured the road but would hold it for just a few weeks before Confederates retook the western portion. Union forces attacked again and recaptured it. They would be in command of the entire line from November 1862 to the end of the war.

The 5-foot gauge Macon & Western Railroad linked the chief rail amenities at Atlanta with Macon's rail center. Nineteen stations lined its 103-mile path. It used 55.5-pound T-rail and was proud holder of at least 19 engines, many built by the esteemed Rogers, Ketchum and Grosvenor and Norris locomotive manufacturers.

In August 1864, the Macon & Western would find itself deeply pitched in the Battle of Jonesboro. Sherman had been trying to take Atlanta for a month with little success. His foe, John Bell Hood, had been using the M&W as a lifeline for his Army of Tennessee. Sherman decided to cut the line. He marched on August 25 and four days later took a position on high ground within several miles of the railroad. Confederates responded by massing just west of Jonesboro. Fighting broke out and Sherman successfully broke the line forcing the Confederates to retreat. Meanwhile 60,000 Union troops massed south of Atlanta causing the Confederates to send needed ordnance and sustenance trains southward from the city for protection. The Rebels took up positions around Jonesboro, which Sherman, in a ferocious onslaught, broke through in a battle that lasted from 4:00 P.M. until sunset.

The 87 miles of Atlanta & West Point track brought Atlanta the agricultural bounty of the fertile southwest as well as manufactured products from a Selma, Alabama foundry. It too used 5-foot gauge track but with a surprisingly light 44.5-pound rail. The railroad, however, invested in superbly machined American type 4-4-0s exclusively from the shops of Baldwin Locomotive Works and Rogers. Among them were the *E. L. Ellsworth*, the *West Point*, and the *Post Boy*. These were sassy high-steppers with 60-inch driver meant for speed. Most freight trains of the day ran at 20-24 miles per hour. Passengers, however, could enjoy the thrilling whirlwind speed of 30 mph. Travel was not without its dangers. The *Mobile Advertiser and Record* printed a notice of a war-related wreck on the Atlanta & West Point line that happened on April 15, 1862.

Newman, Ga. April 16, 1862.
Mr. Editor,

A very destructive smash-up occurred last night, about nine o'clock, four miles south of Newman on the Atlanta & West Point RR, with the foremost train carrying soldiers by this route towards Corinth, Miss. The train was a long one, having twenty-six boxcars and about a regiment of soldiers. Nine of the front box boxes were completely wrecked and thrown off the track. Only one man was killed—Private G. A. N. Greene, of Lincoln County, Tenn. Some twenty-five, perhaps, are wounded, but none are considered dangerous. The wounded are left in Newman—distributed at private houses. The trains are detained here until nine o'clock this morning. Six horses were killed by the accident.

Yours respectfully,
John E. Robinson
Atlanta, Ga Confederacy

The Atlanta & West Point Railroad, with approximately 130 cars and a dozen stations, became a link in the South's 1200 mile through route from the Gulf at Mobile east to Alexandria on the Potomac River. It was essential in elevating Atlanta as a major rail center and was therefore of great concern to Federal military leaders.

Among the important lines supplying the Confederate war effort was the Charleston & Savannah Railroad. The 110-mile system was conceived to link with a planned seaboard route to develop the bounty of the coastal region. The two important coastal cities, Savannah and Charleston, competed to win the status of most important port city but recognized that a union would be good for both. Rogers-built 4-4-0s were used exclusively on the line and most railroad parts were purchased from Tredegar. They ran on the preferred 5-foot gauge and 56-pound T-rail. In 1861, it was the Lowcountry's (the strip of land below sea level extending from the Sand Hills of South Carolina to the coast) most important commercial and transportation route, with links capable of delivering plantation production to the rest of the country had times been different. Its primary cargoes were cotton, rice, hides, corn, and meal.

During the war the railroad became critical in protecting Savannah even while burdened with supplying Confederate troops with food and ordnance. Lee stayed close to the route from November 1861 to March 5, 1862, even setting up his headquarters at Coosawhatchie, not far from the hum of its rails. So vital was the line that Lee initiated construction of a line of earthen fortifications along it stem from Charleston to the Savannah River. These fortifications were later expanded by Lee's successors.

The S&C was involved in both railroad and naval activity when Federal gunboats on the Whalebranch and Coosaw Rivers broke through the Confederate defenses at Port Royal and Seabrook Ferries.

Other actions involving the railroad included a skirmish in May 1862 in the vicinity of Castle Hill Plantation; the Battle of Pocotaligo in October 1862; the Battle of Honey Hill in the vicinity of Good Hope Plantation in November 1864, and the final breaking of the railroad at Point South in January 1865.

Much of its destruction occurred in December 1864 at the hands of Sherman during his March to the Sea when he severed the line to force Confederate general William Hardee to abandon Savannah. His attempt failed but he was back in 1865 and would severely damage the line during his Carolinas Campaign. After the war it was reorganized as the Savannah & Charleston Railroad. The damage to the line was so extensive it would not open to traffic again until 1870.

The problem of finding good men—not just engineers, but men who could keep a line up and running—plagued virtually all railroads, north and south, from the elegant New York Central to the lowliest rust bucket short line chugging along the edge of a tobacco plantation. Lack of manpower was a constant gripe in correspondences. B&O president John W. Garrett continually lamented how scarcity of workers slowed down the massive repairs and reconstruction required after Stonewall's destructive attacks. The following plea to acquire a capable railroad man illustrates the desperation of Confederate railroad men:

Engineer Bureau
December 9th '62
General S. Cooper
Adjutant and Inspector General C.S.A.
General,

I have just received a communication from George G. Hull, Esq. Superintendent of the "Atlanta & West Point R. Rd." Georgia. In which he states, "I am short of hands, and that too just when the requisitions of the Government are more urgent than ever before. My deficiency is in Engine runners. I need not state how much greater is the necessity to have competent men to manage such machines when every days use is making them, or rather, bringing them nearer the point of actual disability, without the power to get, within the limits of the C. States, the material necessary to make repairs and keep them up to working point. There is one of my old engine men, now in the 7th Georgia Regiment—William Glen—who is fully posted as to my road and engines and grades and schedules. His services are much needed and will much assist us in keeping up the working capacity of the Road. I am pressed every day to the extent by the demands of the Government for transportation of public supplies and I dare not trust my machinery to inexperienced hands. It is wearing out rapidly day-by-day, and therefore it is the more important to the Government that this same machinery should be "conserved" to the utmost. I cannot, at this time, find competent men here to run my engines.

The engine driver I want, William Glen, 7th Georgia Regiment, was in the first battle of Manassas and has never been absent a single day from his Regiment since. He does not know of my application for his services.

The Atlanta & West Point R. Road is a part of the only line between Richmond and the Mississippi Valley also between Chattanooga and the valley. It is essential to R. Road communication between the different commands in the Western Department. The good of the service requires that the man should be detailed for the duty named, which I have respectfully to request and ask that he be ordered to report to George G. Hull Esq. At Atlanta, Georgia.
Very Respectfully
Your Obt. Servt.
J. F. Gilmer
Col. Of Engrs. & Chief Engr. Bureau.

Of course many men had entered the military, seeking adventure on land or on the high seas. The Confederacy just didn't have the manpower to do what they wanted. The president of the Central (of Georgia) Railroad authorized the expenditure of $200,000 in 1862 for the purchase of slaves to help with the shortfall in laborers.

A railroad depended on machinists, carpenters, men to move freight from storage sheds to cars or ships, station workers, line workers, masons, stablemen, signalmen, watchmen, foremen, blacksmiths, and maybe a diviner to direct well diggers to a water supply.

Some southern lines fared better. The Richmond & Danville Railroad managed to double its employment by the end of the war but they were among the exceptions. They made due with 519 employees and 700 slaves.

The increased traffic should have been a boon to these railroads but a trend of sloppy management within the Confederate hierarchy prevented this. First of all, an overwhelming 25 percent drop in profits the first year forced railroad companies to lay off workers—men they would desperately need back the next year when things started picking up. But those fellows, many of them skilled carpenters, machinists, tracklayers, and yardmen, entered military service and were killed or gone for the duration of the war.

The Confederate government initially appealed to railroad owners' patriotism, asking them to transport military needs for free. That, of course could not last. When they finally decided to pay them it was with ill-backed government bonds at rates far below what the railroads normally charged for commercial transport. In time suppliers of railroad equipment would not accept the government bonds for payment.

Attempts to court European countries into supporting the Confederacy floundered, especially after Lincoln's Emancipation Proclamation. They certainly did not want to be excoriated for supporting a new slave nation. In response to this perceived slight, the Confederate government refused to buy railroad supplies from overseas. Then they turned around and told railroad owners they could send their agents over to purchase the replacement parts but they would make no special effort to help get those supplies through the Union blockade. Along with this was the diversion of tons of iron, much needed by the railroads, to build ironclads.

With the deck stacked against them, owners had to rely on their own resourcefulness to keep their railroads running. The Confederate government, like the Federal government, realized it was best to let railroads be run by railroad men who knew what they were doing and not send bureaucrats and self-important military officials to breath down their necks.

It was never far from Southern railroad owners' thoughts that their lines were targeted by the powerful USMRR. The thought of engines and equipment lettered United States Military Railroads running down their precious track was unnerving. At least, in many cases, they could count on reasonable protection from the Confederate army.

Much praise is leveled, deservedly, on the efficient operation of the Northern railroads in the war but there are fascinating aspects of Southern railroads that are often overlooked. By the end of the war, for instance, many of the Confederate railroads still had the majority of the engines they started with. They were in questionable shape but still running. It is true that many Southern railroads were in a shambles by the end of the war, both mechanically and financially. Some were worse off than when chartered. They would be restored however. The Union returned ownership of captured and assimilated lines shortly after the war. In light of all this, considering the overwhelming odds against them, it is undeniable that the South often made more efficient use of their railroads than the North.

Construction costs of Southern railroads during the 1850s were often lower than Northern lines especially in regions such as the Lowcountry. Slave labor certainly had an impact on this. Another factor was a more favorable climate. This permitted the laying of ties on bare ground. Fills and long sections of shaped roadbed were tamped firm with the ties then snuggled in. The rail was then spiked in. Expensive ballasting—usually with small or crushed stone—was used sparingly between the ties. Lack of ballasting of course presented its own set of problems. It could take up to two years for the track to firmly settle into the roadbed. Sections of track could slide or shift and there was the constant threat of the dirt beneath the track weakening or being washed away. Track crews were constantly repairing these weak spots and replacing rotted ties or those that fractured from lack of ballast. Using green ties—wood not properly dried—caused flexing and weak spots. The process of soaking ties in creosote to extend their life was being introduced but was, because of cost, a luxury. But no matter what kind of track was laid down, there were always methods to render it useless, and attacking tracks was the simplest and best way to disrupt trains. Destroying tracks, bridges, and other structures was a major strategy for both the North and the South.

The "path of bonfires" commonly used by both sides to destroy railroad tracks was the brainchild of USMRR's Herman Haupt. Ties would be piled tightly and rail would be poised at angles over them. When burned, heat from the pinnacle of the stack would soften the rail causing them to bend. There was no way of repairing them other than through re-rolling at a mill. Rail could be ripped from the track using horseshoe shaped clamps. Invented by E.C. Smeed, the clamps were tapped under one end of the rail while the other end was held firmly in place. Using a sturdy timber fixed to the clamps, applied pressure ripped the rail from the ties. As more pressure was applied, the rail was twisted into a useless length. It was a quick way of wrecking rail, leaving it needing a trip to an iron works for repair.

We have already looked at Haupt's method of using a "torpedo" to bring down a bridge. All these techniques were designed with speed in mind. USMRR raiders could ride out of the woods and wreak havoc on a section of track in a few short hours. Confederate raiders learned fast. They were not ashamed to use these same techniques in their raids.

The defeat of General Rosecrans and his Union forces at Chickamauga in September 1863 caused panic in the War Department. Control of eastern Tennessee was close to being compromised. The response would be an extraordinary and unprecedented use of the railroads.

A war council was called. Attending were President Lincoln, Secretary Stanton, General Halleck, Daniel McCallum, and several other high-ranking military officials. (Haupt had recently been dismissed due to an argument with Stanton.) The logistics of moving a large force to save East Tennessee was discussed. The task of moving 20,000 to 25,000 troops from Virginia to Bridgeport, Tennessee—a distance of 1,200 miles—was

also discussed. Options considered ranged from 40 to 90 days—far too long. After a heated debate, the President and others were left frustrated and dispirited.

Later, T. T. Eckert, Chief of the Telegraph of the Army, was brought in to the discussion. After study of timetables and other relevant considerations with McCallum, it was determined the move could be made by rail in 10 to 15 days. To support their conclusions they referenced a comprehensive report written in February 1862 by then Assistant Secretary of War, Thomas A. Scott.

Lincoln was convinced, wild as it sounded. The plan would constitute one of the largest single movements of troops in the war. The 11th and 12th Corps of Meade's Army of the Potomac—some 20,000 troops—were to be sent to Tennessee, including their artillery and supplies.

Garrett of the B&O was brought in to assist McCallum and other officials in this monumental undertaking. The operation commenced September 25, 1863. The railroads used were the Baltimore & Ohio, Orange & Alexandria, Central Ohio, Indiana Central, Indianapolis, Louisville & Nashville, and the Nashville & Chattanooga. The movement included ferrying soldiers from one line to another where needed.

The 11th Corps at Manassas Junction and the 12th Corps at Brandy Station were rushed to Washington and for three days the new Long Bridge across the Potomac bore the weight of unending train travel. The Federal government was now in control of all railroads involved. All commercial traffic was suspended, preference being given to this enormous military event.

Polished and majestic, USMRR engines glistened as they raced westward beneath the

September sun. At twilight they became darkly imperial, chuffing through the countryside, sparks fluttering from their balloon stacks. Amidst the clanging of bells and whistle blasts, they rolled methodically into rail yards at night, the engineers mindful of the positions of semaphores. The engines, seething and sweating, sparkled in the constant movement of lanterns as men quickly filled their tenders with water and wood while other yardmen greased linkage and journals. Thousands of troops disembarked in orderly fashion, filling the yards before moving to yet another strange railroad.

On October 8, 1863, the last of the 23,000 troops arrived at their base 26 miles from Chattanooga—a remarkable 14 days after the movement began. It was not without its problems and bickering but it was a triumph that deeply impressed Lincoln. Moreover it was a testimony to the cooperation between railroads in an hour when their country needed them.

The movement would not be surpassed. A similar movement of the 23 Corps from Tennessee to Virginia in January of 1865 would come close. It would not even be rivaled during the massive demobilization after the war when hundreds of thousands of troops were returned to their homes.

This "grand piece of strategy," the transport of the 11th and 12th Corps, was a major accomplishment of the USMRR. Another one lay ahead, however. A wrathful storm was about to be unleashed on a bitter southern enemy. The mechanics of which had been accumulating quickly in the mind of General William T. Sherman.

An engine and car stand on the trestle over the Little River in North Carolina. The Atlantic & North Carolina car is lettered Conductor's Car No. 1 and is probably a commissary car, bringing supplies to Union soldiers protecting the bridge. There is a water tank at the end of the bridge where water was pumped from the river for locomotives. Keeping engines fueled was a challenge. Wood fuel was another matter. Nearly every station had wood ricks. Prior to the war, farmers were paid to leave piles of chopped wood along the track. (*Author's Collection*)

Boxcars and fresh wheels are ready for shipment at the James River docks opposite Richmond, Virginia. (*Library of Congress*)

Engine #153 of the USMRR stands boldly at City Point. A company of infantry is to the right. In the background is the blockhouse built to defend the rail yard (see page 167). (*National Archives*)

A Federal salvage crew has another mess to clean up, delivered at the hands of bold Rebels. This time a wrecking train has been sent to a location on the Alexandria, Loudon & Hampshire Railroad. Workers strain to roll damaged wheels onto a flatcar. (*National Archives*)

The junction of the Alexandria, Loudon & Hampshire Railroad and the Alexandria & Washington Railroad is under Federal control in this Andrew J. Russell photograph. (*Library of Congress*)

Fabricating bridge spans was not a new concept. The B&O had iron Bollman spans manufactured and shipped piecemeal by rail to sites in ante-bellum days. The assembled trusses pictured at top are stored in the Alexandria lumberyard. (*Library of Congress*) This rare view, below, shows the forms inside the lumber shop at Alexandria over which timbers were bent and laminated to shape railroad trusses. (*Author's Collection*)

Contrabands display devices and tools used to bend rail. (*Library of Congress*)

A portable assembly was engineered to straighten track. Using sturdy blocks and a jack, bends in rail of a foot or less could be repaired. (*Library of Congress*)

Prisoners at Andersonville Prison gather in the mess line. The horrendous living conditions and high mortality rate at the prison in Andersonville, Georgia, have been well documented. Approximately 45,000 men were imprisoned here between February 1864 and April 1865. The majority were brought by railroad from Virginia. The railroads used included the Richmond & Petersburg, Raleigh & Gaston, North Carolina, Augusta & Savannah, and the Central of Georgia. Prisoners and their guards arrived in groups of 600 aboard boxcars (prison cars) with the trains being held over for several days. Supplying the prison greatly strained Confederate railroads in the region. (*National Archives*)

Deep within the photograph of the union camp at Culpeper Court House (see page 138) is this scene of railroad activity where two locomotives are involved in Union troop movements. Professional Civil War-era cameras could capture amazing detail. This spot is nearly a mile from where the photographer took the picture. (*Library of Congress*)

A Federal supply train is unloaded beside a warehouse at Culpeper Court House. (*Library of Congress*)

A row of bonfires along a section of track simmers in the twilight. A soldier waits patiently for the stacked ties to heat the rails sufficiently to warp them. (*Library of Congress*)

The *W. H. Winton* stands majestically with her proud crew on the swing section at the end of Washington's Long Bridge. This was one of two machines named W. H. Winton built during the war by different manufacturers. This one was built by Mason. (*Author's Collection*)

Development of the Federal base at City Point continues near the James River docks. In the lower left of the photo is evidence of the massive ever-expanding fill needed to support larger warehouses such as the one beside the locomotive. (*Library of Congress*)

A new turntable awaits use in the shadow of the City Point engine house. (*Library of Congress*)

A coal train pulls away from the City Point engine house while switching and loading operations continue near the docks. (*National Archives*)

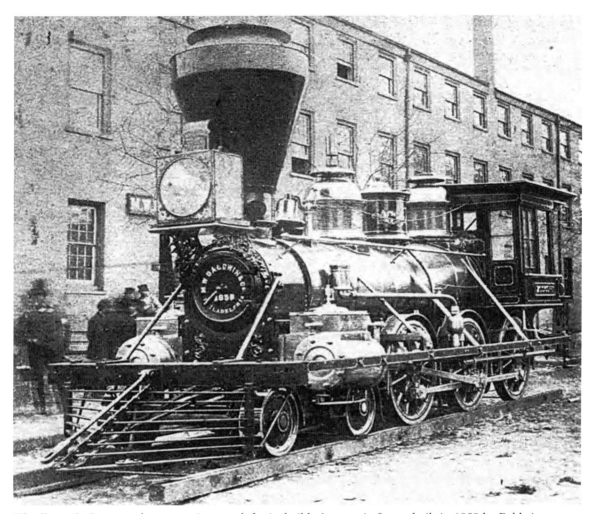

The *James S. Corey* stands on strap iron track for its builder's portrait. It was built in 1859 by Baldwin Locomotive Works for the South Carolina Railroad. The powerful 10-wheeler has a supplementary outside frame, beautiful domes, and a Russian iron boiler jacket. This stern fellow would see service along Deep South cypress swamps where its strap iron cowcatcher was likely to encounter large alligators warming themselves on the tracks. (*Author's Collection*)

Engine 133 of the USMRR stands impressively in front of the thickly fortified, multi-towered blockhouse at City Point. The engine crew waits patiently for the duration of the photographer's exposure. Overall, engine crews were even tempered. There was a deep kinship between them since their lives depended on cooperation. It was a dangerous life for conductors both North and South. Often starved and exhausted during runs, they had to worry about being shot through the cab window by a sharp shooter or having their engine derailed or sent into a river because the bridge was destroyed. If all that weren't enough, the water at City Point was of poor quality leading to outbreaks of typhoid. They were in a light mood when this photo was taken. They put flower pots along the engine walkway. (*Library of Congress*)

This interesting detail was drawn out of a larger image of Big Black River Station, Mississippi, at top, taken by photographer William Pywell Redish. Union soldiers on the lawn of a residence watch a Southern Railroad train bound for Vicksburg rumble through a cut. The Southern was an example of a railroad nearly burnished out of existence by the war. Confederates destroyed the railroad's Big Black River bridge leaving a mere 12 miles of operable track between the river and Vicksburg. (*Library of Congress*)

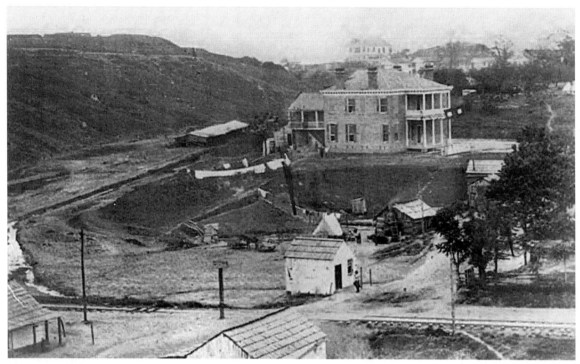

This picturesque location at a railroad crossing in Vicksburg, Mississippi, served as the U.S. Signal Corps headquarters during the Union occupation. (*Library of Congress*)

Switching operations are underway at the yard and station in Warrenton, Virginia. This spur off the Orange & Alexandria main stem would suffer great damage by both sides. (*Library of Congress*)

A dramatic eyewitness rendering by Alfred R. Waud shows a train falling into the Chickahominy River in southeast Virginia. The engine was pulling a train in reverse when it unexpectedly ran over a bridge destroyed by Confederate raiders. Waud used pencil, Chinese white, and black ink wash on brown paper. (*Library of Congress*)

The supply base at Stoneman's Station, Virginia, holds plenty of supplies for the Union Army, including boxes of ammunition, forage, tents, and whiskey. (*National Archives*)

Barges and schooners bring ammunition to the magazine wharf at City Point. (*Library of Congress*)

The *Quigley* was built in 1859 by Moore & Richardson of Cincinnati for the Louisville & Nashville Railroad. The builder was contracted to build a total of five of these appealing locomotives for the railroad. The stack seems disproportionally large for an otherwise simple 4-4-0. The slight angle of the cylinders suggests uncertainty by the builder. (*Author's Collection*)

An ambitious effort was taken up in 1864 by Union General Benjamin F. Butler and men of the Engineer Corps to dig a canal along a severe bend in the James River near Dutch Gap. Confederates were holding back his soldiers at Bermuda Hundred and preventing a Union fleet from moving up the James River to take Richmond. If completed, "Butler's Canal" would have taken care of both of these but the project was abandoned. A small flat car to the left affirms the use of a railroad to haul stone away. (*Library of Congress*)

Looking like a medieval drawbridge, this railroad bridge spanned the Cumberland River in Nashville. In addition to its elevated guard towers, it had heavy doors that could be closed across the tracks in the event of an attack. A closer look at the Nashville bridge reveals it was a swing bridge as well. The center span, given additional balance and strength from overhead tower cables, revolved on a wheeled turret. The small buildings were used by bridge operators. (*Library of Congress*)

Nearly a dozen Union locomotives await assignments in the Nashville & Chattanooga Railroad yard at Nashville's Church Street station. The structure has an exotic look with Moorish arches over the train shed entrances and a battlement roof. The State Capital building is visible in the upper right. (*Library of Congress*)

A small but sturdy blockhouse was built at the vast Nashville & Chattanooga bridge near Whiteside, Tennessee, for the protection of Federal guards. The route was critical to Sherman's supply line. (*National Archives*)

A long train stands precariously atop the fragile looking Nashville & Tennessee trestle spanning Running Water Ravine. This was a hastily constructed span that would be replaced in 1863 by the Construction Corps. (*National Archives*)

A cook in the U.S. Colored Troops prepares soup for railroad workers. (*Library of Congress*)

A Yankee guard stands contemplatively at the entrance of the bridge at Strawberry Plains near Knoxville, Tennessee. A man—most likely the photographer's assistant staging a second photo—is standing to the right beside a large professional stereograph camera on a tripod. Commissioned photographers usually had several cameras and a portable darkroom in their wagon. (*Library of Congress*)

The massive Loudon bridge spanning the Tennessee River was rebuilt by USMRR Construction Corps to replace the bridge destroyed during a Confederate retreat. It carried the tracks of the East Tennessee & Georgia Railroad. (*Author's Collection*)

The cause of this mishap on the Cumberland & Pennsylvania Railroad is not known, but work crews have the monumental task of hauling the Winans-built Camel and its train of iron pot cars out of Willis Creek in Maryland. The railroad was built to haul iron and coal from rich coal seams in western Maryland. Winans specialized in 0-8-0 Camels. They were slow powerful haulers capable of managing the tough grades of Maryland's hilly coal country. (*Author's Collection*)

Lee pulled away from Petersburg during the night of April 2, 1865. With the city lost, he informed President Jefferson Davis in Richmond. The nearly abandoned Capital was already in near ruins when retreating Confederates set fire to railroad buildings, the arsenal, supply warehouses, and industries. The fires quickly joined and ranged out of control threatening to destroy the entire city. Anguished citizens accompanied the mayor to the Union line to first surrender the city and then beg for help in putting out the fires. Union soldiers rode into Richmond down New Market Road and, using fire engines and bucket brigades, helped to extinguish the fires. (*Library of Congress*)

FIVE

A SEA OF RUBBLE

"No tongue can tell, no mind conceive, no pen portray the horrible sights
I witnessed this morning"
—Captain John Taggert, 9th Pennsylvania Reserves, Sept. 17, 1862

It is left to military experts to decide what is a "good" war and which is "bad." Of course the ones you win are good but there is an outlying science to the business. It keeps strategists ever searching through historical records, deducing tips on what brought victory or defeat: generalship, logistical superiority, management, and optimizing tactical advantages. Not that anyone thinks of war as good. It is a phenomenon of the human condition. But there are reasonable ways to fight them and also savagely inhuman ways.

Most wars are a combination of conventional and unconventional tactics, with the latter often serving the grander goals of the former. The use of railroads in the Civil War was certainly unconventional—to the point of making the conventional methods of fighting unimaginably deadly.

Perhaps it is safe to conclude that wars fought in and around cities and towns are roundly bad. Unlike sea battles bravely fought on the lonely ocean or armies colliding on far away plains, wars fought in and around population centers involve more than

soldiers; these wars are wars of children. The fighting comes into their backyards. They huddle in terror at the explosions and bullets coming through windows. Their neighborhoods where they explore and play with friends are destroyed.

They are made orphans. Disease threatens them when the infrastructure of the community is destroyed. And then there is the terror of evacuations and long lines of refugees. Starvation, thirst, sickness, and trauma leave marks that were never supposed to happen in their land.

We know what happened in so many towns during the American Civil War: Sharpsburg, Gettysburg, Shiloh, and dozens of others where troops were railroaded in. After the battle the armies left. Wagon trains of wounded stretch for miles. It was sometimes a combination of blood and iron as engineers eased throttles, reducing the speed of their locomotives to a mere crawl so crewmen could run ahead and remove bodies off track. Burial crews did their best to dispose of the dead with some dignity but all too often the problem was overwhelming. Usually African Americans were set to the gruesome business of gathering up the dead.

Losses of this magnitude were new. Boxcars of coffins quickly became infeasible. Mass graves dug by weary arms became a standard procedure. The stiffened arms and legs of the dead, frozen in vicious death positions were first thoughtfully pressed down but as frustration set in, they were kicked down. Animal carcasses were left to rot, poisoning the air with such terrible stench that townsfolk had to hold rags saturated with balms to their noses. The landscape was left wrecked and littered and a collective trauma gripped townsfolk for months. For years these places had grim distinctions. Children would have to learn that their town was the scene of slaughter because, "the railroad come through here and the Yanks were after it."

The war would soon flow into Southern cities as Federals hunted their rail facilities. If terrible enough, the destruction might psychologically paralyze the citizenry into submission. "War is the remedy our enemies have chosen and I say let us give them all they want," Sherman proclaimed during his March to the Sea. The massive disruption of society he was about to unleash on the South would spawn hatred for generations.

In the first Battle of Fredericksburg, December 11-15, 1862, newly appointed General Ambrose E. Burnside positioned his Army of the Potomac in the natural geographical amphitheater near Fredericksburg. The objective was to take the old city and secure its main road leading to Richmond, the Confederate capital. Lee had not anticipated this. His army had been divided between actions in the Shenandoah Valley

and at Culpeper. Burnside needed to cross the Rappahannock River to get at Fredericksburg. He ordered pontoon bridges be sent to him for the crossing since all existing river bridges had been destroyed. A combination of blunders, bad weather, and miscommunications delayed the arrival, giving Lee time to regroup and rush his army to the city. By late November, Lee was in place with Stonewall Jackson and Longstreet.

Armaments, supplies, and both pontoon and railroad bridge sections started arriving in December by way of the Richmond, Fredericksburg, & Potomac Railroad. The railroad included the recently restored Aquia Creek & Fredericksburg Railroad. A pair of bridges were assembled and then floated up the Rappahannock River. Along the way the engineers came under Confederate gunfire from sharpshooters in homes and yards along the Fredericksburg shore. Repeated attempts to bring the spans into position were met with heavy gun fire.

When the first stages of construction of the railroad bridge were detected, Confederates sent a barrage of shellfire and bullets, killing workers, shattering derricks used to set up the trestle supports, and smashing some of the prefabricated spans. Certain they could find a less stressful way to spend the day other than being exposed to enemy shelling, the workers quickly deserted the area.

A frustrated Burnside ordered his artillery chief, Brig. Henry J, Hunt to blast Fredericksburg. From Stratford Heights, 150 rail delivered guns commenced bombarding the city. In the course of two terror-filled hours, 8,000 shells reigned down on the city.

During the Battle of Fredericksburg, December 11-15 1862, Confederates opened fire on Union soldiers attempting to build pontoon and railroad bridges across the Rappahannock. General Ambrose Burnside responded by having his artillery unit open a barrage on the city using 150 guns. The destruction caused by the artillery bombardment from across the Rappahannock reached deep into Fredericksburg, destroying businesses and residences alike. (*Library of Congress*)

An account recorded by Confederate D. A. Dickert of the 3rd South Carolina vividly describes what happened:

> While the dense fog was yet hanging heavily over the waters, one hundred and forty guns, many siege pieces, were opened upon the deserted city and the men along the water-front. The roar from the cannon-crowned battlements shook the very earth. Above and below us seemed to vibrate as from the effects of a mighty upheaval, while the shot and shell came whizzing and shrieking over-head, looking like a shower of falling mete-ors. For more than an hour did this seething volcano vomit iron and hail upon the city and the men in the rifle pits, the shells and shot from the siege guns tearing through the houses and plunging along the streets, and ricocheting to the hills above. Not a house nor room nor chimney escaped destruction. Walls were perforated, plastering and ceiling fell, chimneys tottering or spreading over yards and out into the streets. Not a place of safety, save the cellars and wells, and in the former some were forced to take refuge.

When it was over the Federal bridge crews re-emerged only to be met with gunfire again. Burnside sent volunteers over in scows to attack the Confederates. Fighting moved down the cobblestone streets and from house-to-house in what would be the first urban combat in the war. On December 12,

Burnside sent reinforcements across to finish the job but they instead rampaged through the city. Saloons must have been sought first. A disgusted Connecticut Chaplain recorded the following:

> I saw men break down the doors to rooms of fine houses, enter, shatter the lookinglasses with the blow of an ax, and knock the vases and lamps off the mantelpiece with a careless swing. . . . A cavalry man sat down at a fine rosewood Piano, drove his saber through the polished keys, then knocked off the top and tore out the strings.

This senseless destruction did little to further Burnside's poorly conceived intentions. The result of the battle, in a nutshell, was a humiliating defeat for the Union. Combined casualties were 8,000. The affable Burnside's inability to dislodge the crafty Lee from the heights behind Fredericksburg was not thwarted by the difficulties of crossing the Rappahannock, but by the treachery of politics.

Lincoln needed a victory to silence his critics—even among his Radical Republicans—and convince an unsettled public that the war was going as planned. The weight of the defeat bore down on him again. "If there is a worse place than Hell than I am in it," he said in the depths of disappointment.

The stalwart folks of Fredericksburg returned to their wrecked city. They settled their panicked children down and set about removing the debris, brick by brick. The proprietors of brickyards would, as coffin makers did, consider barter for payment of services rendered.

In June 1863, General Lee launched his second invasion of the North with his 75,000-strong Army of Northern Virginia. It did not sit well with those Southerners who wanted only to fight a defensive war. They considered the conflict the "War of Northern Aggression." As a result Lee would lose a lot of soldiers through desertion. In early June he moved into Pennsylvania in the general region of Gettysburg although it was not believed the confrontation would be there.

Lee immediately went after the Northern Central Railway, a subsidiary of the Pennsylvania Railroad. Connecting Baltimore with Sunbury, Pennsylvania, it was an important Federal supply route. It had connections with the Gettysburg Railroad via the Hanover Branch Railroad.

When Lee got done with it, 32 bridges along the Northern Central and Hanover Branch were destroyed. Herman Haupt was brought in to supervise repairs and portions of the lines were up and running again in ten days. The audacious actions of Lee and his intent to bring the war north sent shudders along Northern lines servicing the region. They had been unsettled and fearful since May 1863, with the Union defeat at Chancellorsville. Even the important rail facilities at Aquia Creek had to be abandoned. A hurried evacuation got over 500 carloads of supplies and 12,000 wounded out of there.

With Lee in the region, Pennsylvania Railroad officers naturally feared an attack, possibly at Harrisburg. Soldiers were sent to protect the main Pennsylvania Railroad bridges along the line. Haupt even utilized the Western Maryland Railroad, a coal hauling line running through Maryland, West Virginia, and Pennsylvania. It had limited passenger service and ran on strap iron fastened to stringers. It must have run mostly coal burning engines because Haupt had its old wood burners sent off for repair. The line, which usually ran three to five trains a day was, under Haupt's upgrading, running as many as 15 trains daily to supply Meade's army poised for confrontation with Lee.

On July 1, 1863, it was discovered Lee was concentrating his forces at Gettysburg. Once in place Lee threw his full force of 75,054 men against Gen. George G. Meade's 83,289 strong Army of the Potomac. In three days of the bloodiest fighting ever in the Western Hemisphere an estimated 51,000 men would lose their lives. Lee's army was defeated.

The traumatized villagers returned to what was left of their isolated little crossroads. Their countryside had become a canvas to a new art of killing and it showed in gouged fences knocked disturbingly ajar, branches hewn from trees by bullets, littered roads, and ignored dead left for others to bury.

The whole terrible thing challenged their sensibilities about living decent and overall good lives. Their modest churches would fill with worshippers seeking words of hope and understanding. A growing evangelical movement, both North and South, was leading to deeper religiosity in spite of the seeds of doubt sown by Darwinism. In fact, soldiers were growing more religious with each battle. For children, it was the gentle, universal reassurance of loving parents that calmed their trembling.

The Gettysburg railroad station that had drawn boys to watch engines rumble in and out, filling them with thoughts of far away places, had become a hospital—a fearful place of shrieking suffering wounded. Those magnificent train engines were now scary things. They helped bring misery and soldiers who became grisly corpses for their simple rural cemetery. Between July 9 and early August, the station would shelter medics brought in to care for nearly 16,000 fly-harassed, maggot pricked, gangrene-threatened wounded.

It was at this station that arrogant windbags came to expound, sometimes for hours, about the glory of this and that during the dedication of Gettysburg Cemetery. But it was here that President Lincoln arrived before venturing to the cemetery to give a simple address he wrote on the train—a speech he would later say was a personal failure.

Advancements in the Federal Ambulance Corps were put to the test at Gettysburg. By the early morning of the Fourth of July, the day after the battle, not a single wounded Union soldier remained on the field. Wounded were taken to field hospitals in ambulances. Eventually they were brought to the station to await hospital trains to transport them to larger Union hospitals.

Hospital trains were supervised by the Medical Department. The first cars used for transport of sick and wounded were freight and passenger cars. They were ill suited for the needs of patients and hospital staff. The hospital cars brought in to Gettysburg were much improved, having rubber slings that held litters or cots and acted as shock absorbers. This provided some comfort to patients who would otherwise be jostled around by the moving train. Other hospital cars were fitted out with facilities for staff, dressing stations, apothecaries, and operating tables.

A dazed and stricken General Meade watched Lee's 14-mile long wagon train of wounded leave after the battle. Seemingly tapped out of the same mold that cast Lincoln's previous generals, Meade refused to pursue Lee and finish him off. Lincoln was again left bewildered and disgusted. Gettysburg would also be the last operation for the brilliant 46-year-old Herman Haupt. On September 14, 1863, Stanton relieved Haupt of his duties after a contentious face-off in Stanton's office. Haupt shrugged it off. He didn't need the aggravation. Facing him were nightmarish legal and financial problems stemming from Hoosac Tunnel litigation. Brilliant, creative, able to assess and work out problems almost immediately, and undaunted, he would have a productive future.

There was another railroad technology that evolved along with the hospital train but with a far different purpose. The armored railcar was inevitable. Records suggest it was Robert E. Lee who first contemplated such a weapon. He wrote the Confederate Ordnance Department on June 5, 1862. "Is there a possibility of constructing an iron-plated battery mounting a heavy gun on trucks, the whole covered with iron to move along the York River Railroad?"

On June 5, he elaborated on his idea in a letter to Capt. George Minor, Chief of Ordnance and Hydrography.

"The Armstrong gun, if mounted on a field carriage with its supply or projectiles, will be of immense importance to us. Can we not have it in the morning?" Deeper in the letter Lee suggests:

Till something better could be accomplished I propose a Dahlgren or Columbiad on a ship's carriage, on a railroad flat and one of your Navy iron aprons adjusted to protect gun and man. If I could get it in position by daylight tomorrow I could astonish our neighbors. The enemy cannot get up his heavy guns except by railroad. We must block his progress.

Lee would have his armored 32-pounder rail cannon, manufactured in Richmond, by June 22. Confederate General Joseph L. Brent gave an account of the weapon in action when Lee made his flank movement against McClellan in one of the Seven Days Battles in June 1862. The weapon had been delivered to Savage's Station on the Richmond & York River Railroad. Brent wrote:

The iron railway battery was sent out on this road from Richmond, and Maj. Gen. MacGruder, commanding the Confederates at Savage Station, ordered this battery to advance and fire on the enemy.

It moved, propelled by steam, down the track, and passed into a deep cut, and from this cut opened with its 32-pound gun, and burst its shell beyond the first line of the Federals, and over the heads of their reserves, forcing them to shift their position.

About the same time skirmishers of the opposing forces became engaged and the lines of battle were deployed, resting on the right side of the railway.

The Union line was a little beyond the cut from which the railway battery fired, and at right angles to it. If the battery had advanced it would have completely enfiladed the Union line at short range, and must have broken it: but owning to the fact that the side and rear of the battery were open and exposed to the fire of skirmishers, and to the further fact that the field of fire of the gun was limited by its embrasure, the battery could not advance; and as the skirmish fire approached, it withdrew.

These mixed results were encouraging. Armored cars built first on flatcars and then on their own modified chassis would follow although their use appears limited. Few drawings and a handful of photos exist. A massive 14-wheeled armored car was used at Petersburg in 1864.

The Siege of Petersburg would witness another experimental rail-borne monster, the *Dictator*. The 13-inch seacoast mortar weighing 17,000 pounds was cast in 1862 at the Fort Pitt Foundry. Intended for siege work, it was fastened to a reinforced rail car. The *Dictator* was run up to the front on the City Point & Petersburg Railroad. A switch was built into the main stem with a section of curved track constructed along a ravine to accommodate it. The curve gave the crew flexibility in aiming the weapon. The *Dictator* could throw a 218-pound shell about two and a half miles on a black-powder charge of 14 to 20 pounds. The shell itself was packed with gunpowder and was sometimes fused to explode at tree level for maximum damage. The rail weapon played a pivotal role in the siege, firing 218 shells over four months. It smashed bomb-proofs and field magazines easily. Confederate gunners,

determined to enfilade fire along the Union's right, retreated, giving the new war machine wide berth.

Baldwin Locomotive Works built a hybrid-armored car for use on the Philadelphia, Wilmington & Baltimore Railroad. It is believed to have used a six-inch revolving gun. Other attempts included ironclad box-cars with a port cut on each side through which a small cannon was fired. These cars usually had smaller ports that allowed soldiers to fire muskets and small pieces.

In August of 1864 Confederate raiders happened upon an armored train on the B&O. It was comprised of a locomotive and six cars of different configurations using iron cladding and rail attached along the sides. Between the rails were ports for cannon and smaller holes through which infantrymen could shoot.

As frightening an aspect as it may have first presented, the bewildered Confederate raiders were not intimidated. They made short work of it, putting a cannon ball through the locomotive boiler and another through a cannon port. They then piled ties around the entire train and lit them on fire. When done, the armored train was a scorched useless heap.

The end of the third year found a divided nation staggered by war. The North was fed-up with all the blunders; the parade of incompetent generals, the missed opportunities to destroy Confederate armies and hasten the war's end. Lincoln was convinced he and his Republicans were going to be voted out in the upcoming election. The Democrats were running Lincoln's former general, McClellan, against him and he was gaining support with promises of a quick end to the war through a negotiated settlement.

The South was facing reality. Their fortunes changed in 1863 after the defeat at Gettysburg. The bloody defeat at Vicksburg at the hands of Grant and the Army of the West deprived the South of its last stronghold on the Mississippi.

They could not win by defeating the Federals but they might be able to prevail by fighting to a stalemate—in other words, win by not losing. Repeated efforts to take their capital at Richmond had been repulsed. There was still hope.

The war had become a nesting ground of depravity—of swindling, prostitution, and alcoholism. Immigrants were forced into enlisting. Antidraft riots in New York City killed at least 120 people. Northerners attacked and killed African Americans during the riots, blaming them for the conflict.

On the other hand religious orders sent women by trains to nurse the wounded. Some ventured onto battlefields to bring back wounded only to be killed. Orphanages opened. Neighborhoods and societies hosted bazaars and other fundraisers to support families.

The railroad that figured so heavily in early strategies had now become *the* strategy. They were about to have one of their largest challenges. Georgia had always been forward-looking in terms of industry. Atlanta was the second most important city after Richmond primarily because of its massive rail hub and industrial strength.

Lincoln and his generals, Grant and Sherman, were of a single purpose and all seemed to get along with each other. The

Deep South had to be penetrated, beaten, and if that didn't work, terrorized to the point of breaking its spirit. The ability for it to make war had to be crushed. Georgia in particular was to become a canvas across which war's bloody paint would be splashed.

On March 9, 1864, Lincoln made Ulysses S. Grant Commander of all Union Armies. William T. Sherman was given command of the Armies of the Cumberland, Ohio, and Tennessee. Union armies, totaling 120,000 were to advance towards Richmond to engage Lee's 64,000-man Army of Northern Virginia, while Sherman would take 100,000 men on an advance towards Atlanta to battle Joseph E. Johnston's 60,000 strong Army of Tennessee.

The massive coordinated Union campaign was to get under way in May but first the mammoth logistical considerations had to be resolved. Supply lines and bases of operations had to organized. USMRR locomotives were systematically fired and prepared for dispatching.

Quartermasters established huge advance bases at Louisville, Kentucky, and Nashville, Tennessee. Sherman put together another base at Ringgold, Georgia. The open markets of large Northern cities were tapped for supplies and food. Railroads, steamboats, and wagon trains immediately began bringing in tons of provisions to fill acres of newly constructed warehouses.

It was up to Brigadier General Daniel McCallum to coordinate the railroad project. The principle lines engaged were the Western & Atlantic, Louisville & Nashville, and the Nashville & Chattanooga, although a multitude of trunk lines in the region were finding their rails worn down by the effort.

Sherman was not satisfied with the 60 locomotives and 130 cars he had at his disposal so issued orders to *acquire* rolling stock from other railroads. He quickly increased his roster to 100 locomotives and 1,000 cars. To protect his supply line from raiders, he had garrison houses built and troops stationed at vulnerable points along the lines. He threatened quartermasters with punishment if they failed to keep the lines protected, well maintained, and repaired.

The Atlanta Campaign took place from May through September with battles at places like Rocky Face Ridge, Resaca, Adairsville, New Hope Church, and Pickett's Mills. There were numerous operations around Marietta, Georgia, and less-remembered ones at Kolb's Farm, Kennesaw Mountain, and Peachtree Creek. All of it was to culminate in Atlanta. Sherman's attempt to extend his right flank to take the railroad between Atlanta and East Point was stopped by a battle at Utoy Creek, August 5-7, 1864.

Union forces entrenched and remained outside Atlanta until late August. There were deadly encounters that month on the 18th and 19th when Sherman's raiders attacked Rebel supply lines on the Atlanta & West Point Railroad. His raiders also hit Lovejoy's Station on the Macon & Western Railroad. Later, they destroyed Confederate supply depots at Jonesborough arrayed along the M&W. Undaunted, Confederates repaired damage to the railroads and had them running in two days.

Sherman's men would make lightening hits at other railroads linked to Atlanta that were supplying Confederate troops. The Alabama & Tennessee was ruptured at Talladega. The Montgomery & West Point got hit 30 miles south of there. Bridges were burned and track torn up along the Central of Georgia and at the yard of the Gordon branch, nearly 50 freight and passenger cars and four engines were destroyed. This equipment was from the Western & Atlantic and had been sent here for supposed safekeeping by the Confederates.

Sherman would hit this same region hard again in late August when he finally cut Confederate Gen. Hood's supply lines along the Macon & Western RR and the Atlanta & West Point RR. The doomed city of Atlanta became the scene of panic as citizens scrambled to board the last trains out. Union raiders captured a 27-car freight train in the vicinity of Griswoldville. After burning the cars, they opened the throttle on the locomotive and sent it steaming at high speed down the main stem where it slammed into the rear of a passenger train of refugees. Fortunately there were no fatalities.

On September 1, 1864, Confederates abandoned Atlanta but not before blowing up much of the railroad equipment on the night of August 31. Atlanta looked volcanic as Hood's retreating army blew up 28 boxcars loaded with ammunition and ordnance. Fiery palls of red smoke could be seen above Atlanta from deep within surrounding counties. Confederate wounded were packed into passenger cars and sent south to Macon amidst the crashing of burning warehouses.

The desperate, panic-filled fiery night of August 31, the night before Atlanta fell, was the culmination of a relentless siege starting in July when Sherman, determined to slug General Hood out of the city, commenced a punishing bombardment. A fortified railroad defense line extending six miles from downtown Atlanta, southwest to East Point, had been keeping Sherman out. On July 20 he ordered all artillery in range of the railroad to not only bombard the line but the city as well. At the time of the order there were perhaps 3,000 civilians out of a normal population of 20,000, still within the city limits. Brave-souls, they toughed it out by staying in cellars and bombproof dugouts. Even after five weeks of continued bombardment, the circle of fortifications extending 11 miles around the city held Union soldiers out. Not even the night of August 9, when 5,000 shells were fired into the city, did the steadfast Southerners capitulate.

With his troops behind him, Sherman entered Atlanta victoriously on September 2. Union officers made themselves at home, taking up residence in Atlanta's finer residences. It would not take long for the Confederacy to seek out scapegoats among President Jefferson Davis's hierarchy. Everything from cowardice to drunkenness would be leveled at generals, quartermasters, and lesser military personnel. Sherman would relish the honor of telegraphing Washington, DC: "Atlanta is ours and fairly won." Combined casualties for the four-month campaign are estimated at 69,000.

This impressive victory restored the North's confidence in Lincoln and he beat Democrat George B. McClellan in the November 8, 1864 election. Carrying all but three states, he won with 55 percent of the popular vote and 212 of 233 electoral votes. There would be no compromise, no cease-fire—no negotiated settlement. The nation was to be preserved as a whole. Solemn but self-assured, Lincoln told supporters on the day the results were confirmed, "I earnestly

believe the consequences of this day's work will be to the lasting advantage, if not the very salvation, of the country."

Prior to the election, in October, Atlanta's desolation deepened in the cooler days of the Georgia autumn. The population had been banished—forced to seek the mercies of surrounding communities. Sherman had every railroad and industrial structure burned. The city hadn't stopped smoldering since it fell.

Sherman was mildly perplexed by Hood's inaction. He knew he was out there, his army reasonably intact and perhaps providing a glimmer of hope for eager Georgians.

It turned out Hood had taken his Army of Tennessee north after the fall of Atlanta with plans to attack the Western & Atlantic, still supplying Sherman. Hood sent corps under Lt. Gen. Alexander P. Stewart to attack garrisons and damage track from October 2 to October 4. Another division was sent with orders to destroy the base where Western & Atlantic rails passed through a deep gap in the Allatoona Mountains and then move north with hopes of destroying the railroad bridge spanning the Etowah River. Sherman rushed men to support the small Federal brigade protecting the railroad at Allatoona Pass. A heated battle ensued October 5 with a two-hour bombardment and heavy fighting at Fort Star, located along the western side of the railroad line. The Federals were pinned down, but because of a false report that a larger Federal force was approaching, the Confederates ended the fighting and retreated. It was over by two o'clock that afternoon. It was a short but deadly battle with 706 Union casualties and 897 Confederate.

Union General John M. Corse, who had commanded both brigades during the battle, took a bullet through the face. The next day he sent Sherman a message, "I am short a cheek bone and one ear, but I am able to lick all hell yet."

In Atlanta on November 11, soldiers began torching private buildings. Soldiers were then ordered to destroy all of the city's railroads. They tore up track, twisting rail into useless spirals or warping it over fire. All remaining depots, warehouses, water towers, engine houses, machine shops, foundries, and storage sheds were burned or blown up. A special battering ram was built to smash down the impressive Car Shed with its distinct monitor along the barrel roof. Atlanta was a shambles, its infrastructure and transportation system in ruins.

On November 15, 1864 the sometimes-insecure Sherman, his swagger back, launched his punitive March to the Sea with 62,000 of his most seasoned troops. "I can make Georgia howl!" he would proclaim. It was to be a personal romp—a terrorizing attack, approved by Lincoln and Grant who weren't totally sure what he was up to. Sherman had all railroads in the vicinity of Atlanta destroyed and then cut off his communications with the North. McCallum dispatched various branches of the Construction Corps to repair and make ready railroads in Savannah, Goldsboro, the Nashville–Decatur line, and facilities at Newbern, North Carolina.

By this time embittered Southerners, their railroads ragged, their economy collapsed by inflation, dealt with the shattered hopes of preserving their former culture. They did not have the resources to resist in any meaningful way what they believed was a cruel if not maniacal onslaught.

Sherman would lay waste a swath 60 miles wide and 300 miles long from Atlanta to the raucous coastal town of Savannah where blockade runners put in to distribute their precious cargoes. One objective was to make war on the people themselves, destroying their towns, cities, farms, and industries. The primary mission, however, was to destroy railroads still capable of supporting the South.

Hood moved North, giving Sherman wide berth but he remained vengeful. He destroyed 20 miles of track between Resaca and Tunnel Hill. Although Sherman figured Hood was still a threat, he was still bent on his own pursuits and so let the Confederate army drift ever westward towards Tennessee where someone else could deal with it.

The USMRR sent Construction Corps to repair the damaged W&A so that wounded could be transported out of Atlanta and supplies could arrive. Determined to rough it with his men on their march, Sherman had Federal workers destroy his own supply line—or a good part of it. Nearly 90 miles of Western & Atlantic track were torn up between Atlanta and Resaca. Railroad stations, telegraph offices, and fuel depots were burned or blown up.

With his army of "bummers" who committed almost heartily to living off the land, Sherman ploughed deeper south. An estimated 300 miles of Southern railroad would be destroyed with almost surgical precision. Sections of the Georgia Railroad would have only naked roadbed remaining as nearly 140 miles of its main stem were destroyed. Any cars Sherman's troops came upon were burned down to their trucks. Locomotives were damaged beyond repair. Rail was warped by fire and then twisted into utterly useless strips. Horses were harnessed to rails and then urged to pull them against trees, causing severe bends. The Macon & Western would suffer severe damage wherever it crossed Sherman's path, as would the Charleston & Savannah, the Southwestern, and the Atlantic & Gulf. Bridges were sent collapsing in flames into rivers and creeks or were blown apart with artillery. A single cannon ball from a small field piece fired at the appropriate angle through trestle piers could bring the whole span down.

Averaging as many as 30 miles a day, Sherman wrecked everything else in his path, sending raiding parties to pillage, rob, harass, and burn. When Sherman reached Savannah on December 21, 1864, he telegraphed Lincoln, offering him Savannah as a Christmas present.

After the war Sherman would admit to having studied accounts of the Clinton-Sullivan Expedition Against the Iroquois in 1779 while preparing his march. In that campaign, General Washington sent nearly 4,000 Continental soldiers and militia into central New York to destroy Indian villages located along the Finger Lakes. Indian cooperation in British–Tory raids against frontier settlements brought this wrath upon them. Entire villages were destroyed. Crops and orchards were wiped out, the trees being cut below ground level to prevent regeneration. Long lines of Iroquois refugees moved northwest to British Fort Niagara expecting the commanders to house and feed them. Unfortunately the fort could barely support the garrison stationed there. Hundreds of Iroquois died along the Niagara River that winter. In the spring entire families were

found dead in caves along the Niagara Escarpment. Sherman had done his homework well. Thousands of Southerners would be condemned to terrible suffering as a result of his rampage.

The Atlanta Campaign and Sherman's subsequent march constituted the greatest achievement of railroads in the entire war. An army of 100,000 men and 60,000 animals (horses, mules, and oxen) was supplied by a single rail line that ran 360 miles through enemy country. Sherman, in his memoirs, was generous in his praise of the railroads involved.

The Atlanta campaign would simply have been impossible without the use of railroads from Louisville to Nashville—185 miles—from Nashville to Chattanooga—151 miles—and from Chattanooga to Atlanta—137 miles. . . . But as I have recorded that single stem of railroad supplied an army of 100,000 men and 35,000 horses for the period of 196 days, viz: from May 1 to November 12, 1864. To have delivered that amount of forage and food by ordinary wagons would have required 36,800 wagons, of six mules each, allowing each wagon to have hauled two tons twenty miles a day, a simple impossibility in such roads as existed in that region of the country. Therefore I reiterate that the Atlanta campaign was an impossibility without those railroads; and only then because we had the men and means to maintain and defend them, in addition to what were necessary to overcome the enemy.

Some interesting first-hand railroad observations were left for us in the diary of Clark Otis who was with Sherman, variously, from December 1863 to July 1864. He was 23 years old when he enlisted in Elmira, New York, leaving his pregnant wife and a small child behind so that he could serve his country. He recounts leaving on the "Lake Shore Road," the Lake Shore & Southern Railroad, from Buffalo, New York, to Cleveland and then on to Indianapolis. After spending time at barracks at Nashville, he was then transferred to Stevenson, Alabama. On Christmas day 1863, he wrote of his harrowing train ride:

> I am feeling blue enough today and I see no reason why I should not feel so here. We are in a totally dark hole. Have to burn candles all-day and suffering from the cold. Yesterday 5 froze to death riding on the cars on account of not having any fire.

A musician able to play several instruments, he was placed in the regimental band. Clark had many difficulties with his bandleader, Mr. Bowen, who was a terrible drunkard. There were daily drunken "sprees" involving other band members. Not being a drinker, Clark comments on the regular drunkenness but appears happier when talking about the many times he gets to play his music—even if it is often spoiled by drinking. When officials arrived at camp from surrounding depots, they would be welcomed with a "serenade" that all too often deteriorated into what Clark called a "circus." He would endure all this while being heartsick for his pregnant wife "Maty" and anxious for letters from home. While encamped, the musical unit was increasingly called out to play for funerals. Wednesday March 16th, 1864, he writes, "Still cold as ever. Played for two funerals. Our instruments froze up twice. It is thought that we will move to the front by quite a good number."

Clark Otis was a member of the musical unit that accompanied Sherman on his march. His diary was filled with interesting railroad stories. He recorded on his ride from Buffalo to Nashville during January 1864, "Yesterday 5 froze to death riding on the cars on account of not having any fire." (*Courtesy Sherlee Ruth*)

The next day he remarked on Confederate raider attacks on a railroad supply line:

> The trains were delayed some 10 hours by Bush-whackers burning two cars—tearing into the track and a bridge." They moved variously by train and by foot. "The (wagon) train was 6 miles along me. Marched till 9 P.M. Our train did not come up so we lay out on the ground.

The band was at the head of the army, playing music. After the Battle of Resaca in Georgia, they were moved to the back of the line. They proceeded through the northwest corner of Georgia, passing through or by Dalton, Lafayette, Calhoun, Adairsville, Cassville, and then on to Marietta. Things got deadlier along the way as his band was sent with the brigade that was involved in fighting at Resaca and the Battle of Allatoona. "Our boys are being badly cut up.

Aril (Ariel?) was wounded through the lung. There is hopes of him. I was homesick. Anything that comes from home makes me feel as though I could not stay away any longer." He and other members of the band were assigned to tend to the wounded brought to field hospitals. He helped remove dead from the battlefield as well. While assisting orderlies with wounded soldiers, he made a promise to God that if he survived the war he would study medicine and become a doctor.

On Wednesday June 22, 1864, he reports, "News come today that the Allatoona Bridge was burnt so that our communications are cut off."

It wasn't until July 4, 1864, that they came near Atlanta, "Hot as ever. The Rebs are about 2 miles off. Can see their breastworks plain," and then on July 5, he "came in sight of Atlanta."

Sherman had brought them to the edge of the city when Otis wrote on July 23:

Still hot. Our forces are working up in good order and the Jonnies will either have to get or get bugged. Our siege guns come up tonight. General Thomas sent in for an unconditional surrender. If they would not submit, he should commence sieging. Before the morning the big guns was heard to roar.

The bombardments continued day and night. Then, on September 2, he writes, "The downfall of Atlanta at 1 P.M. The surrender was made to the 10 NY and 111 PV. We had orders to march, which we did. Got into the city about midnight. A heavy march." On Sunday the 11th, he proudly records, "I am attending church & playing the organ in the 2nd Presbyterian Church.

This is the first service held in the city. A good congregation is present."

On Saturday, November 5, 1864, he writes wearily, "Again on another campaign this P.M. 2 o'clock. Orders came to fall in or pack up and fall in which we did in a hurry. The idea was that we were going to Savannah." Subsequent entries increasingly refer to his fatigue and lameness. In time he stops making entries, possibly too weak or ill to do so. He would survive the war and return to his beloved Maty. And he would keep his promise of becoming a doctor. In 1867, after studying in Rochester, New York, he moved his family to Honeoye Falls, New York where he provided medical service to the community for nearly two decades. He died in 1918.

From Savannah Sherman swung south into the Carolinas. In February, he split his troops, sending half towards South Carolina's capital at Columbia and the other half towards Charleston following the Charleston & Savannah Railroad. Rail was methodically ripped up, warped over fire and, as Sherman would report, "twisted as crooked as a ram's horn."

A method his men employed in destroying track involved prying entire sections up, using crowbars, posts, and hitched-up horses to pull the section over. This in itself would loosen everything. The rail was then pried apart, the ties stacked and fired, and the rail laid over the top. When heat had sufficiently softened the center of the rail, men on either side would pull down, bending the rail to at least a 45 degree angle or more.

The railroad folk in Charleston, knowing Sherman was on his way with the South Carolina Railroad his primary target, sent engines and cars over the North Eastern Railroad and the Cheraw & Darlington to safety. They were right. After Sherman left the city, most of its railroads and attendant structures were in ruins.

The path of fire continued. Citizens abandoned their towns sometimes within the hour Sherman torched them. Their precious railroads, along with gin mills, bridges, and factories were demolished. Other regional railroads hit were the Greenville & Columbia, the Spartanville & Alston, Charlotte & South Carolina, the Wilmington & Manchester, Cheraw & Darlington, Kings Mountain Railway, and North Eastern. In most cases all of them had their railroad stations blown up, bridges demolished, their yards, shops, and facilities destroyed along with any remaining cars and engines.

Simply put, most of the railroads in this region—many dating back to the 1830s—were wiped out. With the restrictions and political wrangling during Reconstruction, it would take decades for them to come back. It must also be noted that many towns and cities were destroyed in all this, sending panicked citizens fleeing from their homes. The countryside became filled with hungry stricken folk who could only look on helplessly as their world was turned upside down.

Confederate Gen. Hood, after scampering away from Atlanta, came up with a grand notion of linking his Army of Tennessee with Lee's Army of Northern Virginia and taking Washington, DC, thus ending the war. His plan collapsed in shambles when his 23,000-man army was rendered impotent after a crushing defeat at Nashville in December 1864. Lee's army and Johnston's forces were all that was left to fight for the South. It was a nearly impossible situation since Northern forces had swelled to 280,000 men in the meantime. But Lee had overcome impossible odds before.

The immediate task was preventing the fall of Richmond. Beyond its significance as the seat of power, it housed a massive Confederate arsenal and the vital Tredegar Iron Works situated along the James River.

During the winter Grant sent teeth-chattering soldiers out of their trenches into seemingly pointless skirmishes. Did Robert E. Lee, during that barren March of 1865, for a moment reconsider his original decision to side with his beloved Virginia? Ultimately his allegiance only brought the state untold suffering. Had he sided with the North, his military genius may have shortened the war by years. The war had *made* him. Now he was considered a murderous traitor in the North and a god-like icon in his broken homeland.

Prior to the war, he had strongly urged the South against secession. Apparently he secretly loathed slavery. When his father-in-law died in 1857, the Arlington slaves were freed as stipulated in the will with no dispute.

Robert and his wife Mary Anna Randolf Custis Lee, inherited magnificent Arlington House. Mary Anna, great-granddaughter of Martha Washington, was repulsed by slavery but believed a mass emancipation would be bad for the country. Now her husband was fighting a Union army with black regiments.

Robert thought often of his gentle wife, tormented by thoughts of her suffering from chronic rheumatoid arthritis and being forced to leave Arlington for safety. She had to secretly move from one quiet location to another in the Richmond vicinity. The Lees would share grief over the loss of their daughter, Annie, who died during the war.

There would be time for healing later. The sight of distant exhaust plumes from USMRR engines dissipating over farm fields as they sped towards Petersburg reminded Lee of the vast challenge confronting him. He was up against Grant again. They had met in a series of hard fought battles in the Overland Campaign in the spring of 1864. That was when Grant first tried to take Richmond but Lee bloodied him at Cold Harbor, driving him away. The defeat persuaded Grant he could not take Richmond by direct assault.

After Cold Harbor, Grant moved his army across the James River and positioned it around Petersburg. Taking this key city would open the door to Richmond, only 25 miles to the south. Petersburg had become the primary supply center for the Confederacy's capital.

What ensued was a long miserable ten-month siege—the longest of the war. Grant's men began digging trenches, slowly encircling Petersburg, and stretching Lee's army ever thinner as they followed. Attacks on both cities occurred regularly, making matters worse for the defenders. Little by little siege guns and rail-borne mortars chipped away. A sea of rubble grew block by block. As the situation became hopeless, people hurried to the depots to catch trains out of both cities.

It was not a siege in the true sense. Grant endured criticism for his lack of aggression but it may have been that he wanted to keep Lee tied up in his defense of Petersburg. In

doing so, Sherman was allowed to savage Atlanta and and continue his rampage to Savannah. Surely Lee, a deeply honor-minded man, must have been disgusted by Sherman's fiendish and uncourageous attack on innocent civilians. Given the chance he would have forcefully challenged him and possibly beat him into retreat. If nothing else he would have sent Sherman north with likely victories, but won at high price.

As mentioned in a previous chapter, an enormous base was developed at the waterfront town of City Point, Virginia, with the purpose of supplying Grant's army during the siege of Petersburg. Trains rolled in and out around the clock, bringing food and supplies to 100,000 troops and forage for 65,000 horses and mules. During intervals between loading and unloading, engineers compared notes. Some used small pocket whistles carved from bone to communicate while in the yard. A brotherhood had developed.

The same was true among captains of the armada of steamboats, transports, barges, and schooners mooring at the eight new wharves. The ignored drovers who brought in wagon trains of supplies surely spoke, over cigars, of the faithful service of their horses, mules, and oxen.

As Grant's trenches expanded, tracks followed. Stations were built at intervals with long sidings and run-around tracks so empty trains could pull off the main stem and let priority ones race to the front. Strict timetables and telegraph communications allowed for uninterrupted movement of nearly 20 daily trains.

Southern railroads that serviced Richmond and Petersburg were, of course, having a terrible go of it. Their majestic bridges of stone, wood, and iron—even some with beautiful Greek Revival covered bridge spans—were left in ruins as USMRR Construction Corps, masters of building and repair, now applied their talents of destruction. The once prestigious railroads being torn apart were the Richmond, Fredericksburg & Potomac, the Richmond & Danville, the Virginia Central, the Richmond & Petersburg, the Richmond & York River, the Norfolk & Petersburg, the Weldon, and the South Side. Most of these lines had been grievously handicapped by earlier assaults. What fragments remained did what they could to get supplies to troops and help citizens evacuate the cities.

The brooding *Dictator* continued to rumble along its isolated siding, bellowing at regular intervals. Its 200-pound shell arched over Petersburg with a steadily increasing whistle, certainly distressing to anyone within earshot. That particular clinking of bricks scattering onto cobblestone streets—a thoroughly defeating sound—followed the explosion.

By October 1864, Grant had successfully cut off the Weldon Railroad, a vital supply line. During the miserable winter, Lee had spread his line of defense almost 37 miles around Petersburg to counter Grant. It was becoming painfully clear to Lee that the intent was to stretch his line thin, making it vulnerable to either a lunge around the Confederate's right flank or a break somewhere else. Grant had been feeling along the line looking for a soft spot to punch through if his opportunity to outflank Lee didn't come.

In a bold move typical of Lee, the Confederates launched a surprise attack on Grant but were defeated in the Battle of Fort Stedman. Tasting victory, Grant sent Gen. Philip Sheridan to capture the South Side Railroad—the last remaining line into Petersburg. Sheridan succeeded at Five Forks, April 1, 1865, busting through the Confederate line and gaining control of all tracks extending to Richmond and other bases. On April 2, Lee's right flank would crumble under a massive assault. Lee immediately withdrew to Fort Gregg, otherwise another episode of urban combat with street fighting would have unfolded. The city was lost. Lee evacuated Petersburg during the night of April 2, 1865.

When word reached Richmond, President Jefferson Davis, his Cabinet, and Confederate defenders immediately abandoned the city during Evacuation Sunday. Certain that Richmond would fall, Davis and his officials hurried towards the last remaining rail line out of the city, the Richmond & Danville, where they boarded a waiting train and headed south. Retreating Confederates moved through the industrial section of the mostly abandoned city, setting fire to their remaining supply warehouses, factories, and rail facilities. The fires quickly joined and ranged out of control, threatening to consume the entire city. The next day desperate citizens accompanied the mayor to Union lines massed east of Richmond. Accepting of their fate, they dutifully surrendered the city and then pleaded with their conquerors to help save what was left. Moved by their plight, Union soldiers mounted their horses and galloped down New Market Road towards the growing plumes of smoke. They entered the city and, using fire engines and bucket brigades, helped to extinguish the raging fires.

An article in the *Richmond Whig*, dated April 12, 1865, explained the situation.

> In our list of losses by the fire, republished this morning, we wish to add what should have been in the first day but for the difficulties under which we labored. They are: Public Warehouse, in which was stored a very large quantity of tobacco; the Richmond and Petersburg Railroad bridge; the Richmond and Danville Railroad bridge, two spans of which were destroyed; Mayo's passenger bridge, which was owned by E.C. Mayo. These were all public losses, not felt alone by the owners, for they affected all classes of the community. It is remarkable that this fire swept away almost every vestige of the Confederate Government from our city.

President Lincoln was brought by train from City Point to the fallen capital on April 4. He solemnly toured on foot the smoldering city with his son Tad and officials. The party then carefully navigated rubble-strewn streets between precariously standing brick walls, eventually reaching the Confederate White House. Lincoln, with "a serious, dreamy expression," sat at Jefferson Davis's desk, briefly. There may have been a quip or two from him, primarily to reassure Tad who was probably unsettled by all the destruction. Later, with his hand on Tad's shoulder, they would visit the Virginia State Capitol.

A week would pass before Lee's inevitable surrender to Grant on April 9, 1865. It came after his rail supply line was cut during the Battle of Appomattox Courthouse. Within that same week, Lincoln would be dead.

It will never be fully known what Lincoln planned to say and do for the reunited nation, but it surely would have been fair, healing, and most likely brilliant. He was taken in the hour he was needed most. An outline of his plans were pursued by his successor, President Johnson, but the nuances had been extinguished by a half-ounce bullet fired from John Wilkes Booth's pistol. There are surgeons today who claim if it happened now he almost certainly could have been saved but his capacity to continue as President would have been unlikely.

As for Reconstruction, Lincoln would have insisted on immediate citizenship for blacks, including all the rights that go along with it. They lost their most important advocate in him. He was killed after a fight to free the slaves. Certainly he would not have permitted the treatment they received afterwards. Perhaps the vengeful, racist policies which condemned the South to nearly a century more of economic and social upheaval could have been avoided.

In some ways, Robert E. Lee's sensible and reassuring words took the place of the martyred President's in calming the still fiery souls of many Southerners who wanted to fight on. In his own way he would expound on the essence of Lincoln's second inaugural address:

> With malice toward none, with charity for all, with firmness in the right as God gives us to see the right, let us strive on to finish the work we are in, to bind up the nation's wounds, to care for him who shall have borne the battle and for his widow and his orphan,

to do all which may achieve and cherish a just an lasting peace among ourselves and with all nations.

Lee thoughtfully encouraged a realistic path. He entered private life, becoming President of Washington College in Lexington. But the war had ravaged Lee. He died five years later. Mary Anna would visit her ancestral home at Arlington one more time. Confined to a wheelchair, she was troubled by it having become a cemetery. She would die nearly destitute.

In his final report, McCallum would detail the massive undertaking of the USMRR. Among the points he recorded were the facts that 2,100 miles of road were operated and that 419 locomotives were used in the transport of 6,330 cars with overall expenditures estimated at 30 million dollars.

With the end of the war, railroads would have some of their heaviest travel through demobilization as hundreds of thousands of troops were returned home. At depots across the country, church and neighborhood organizations waited for trains to arrive. They then boarded coaches, providing water and food to soldiers. There were of course thousands of amputees. When possible, their bandages were removed, the stumps tended and then rewrapped with fresh bandages. The most impaired would be helped to other railroads to make connections.

There was to be a more solemn mission ahead for some railroads as they transported the martyred President from Washington to Springfield, Illinois.

Confederate soldiers let a Union photographer take this photo from the railroad bridge into Fredericksburg during a break in fighting. The large levers at the end of the track indicate there was a drop section to allow passage of riverboats. (*National Archives*)

Confederates destroyed the Richmond, Fredericksburg & Potomac Railroad bridge over the Rappahannock during the Federal siege of Fredericksburg. The photo was taken immediately afterwards indicated by the still smoldering timbers. (*Library of Congress*)

The major rail center at Atlanta was about to feel the wrath of Sherman. He would launch his punitive March to the Sea from the city but first all rail facilities had to be destroyed. Confederate General Hood did his part when he abandoned the city, blowing up storehouses and ammunition cars. When Sherman began his bombardment, remaining citizens rushed to the massive Car Shed in the background to board the last trains out of the city. Sherman's men would build a battering ram and use charges to bring down the impressive structure with its large distinct roof. (*Library of Congress*)

The corner of the Atlanta train shed is to the right in this view of the railroad intersection. The Concert Hall stands in the background. (*Library of Congress*)

The image above and the one opposite were enlarged from the photograph at top of the Atlanta railroad yards. Here, an old locomotive demoted to yard duty simmers on the track outside the Atlanta Car Shed. The crossing house on the left was used by a crossing guard who directed pedestrians safely from one side of the tracks to the other. (*Library of Congress*)

The crew of the *Washington* were engaged in switching operations at the Atlanta yard when the photo was taken. (*Library of Congress*)

This devastation in Atlanta came at the hands of the Confederates on August 31, 1864, when they blew up 28 cars loaded with ammunition and ordnane as they abandoned the city. The chimneys are all that is left of Schofield Rolling Mill. A terrible crash occurred during the confusion of the Rebel evacuation. A train loaded with wounded was sent steaming south towards Macon when it collided head-on with a commissary train. An estimated 30 men were killed and many more grievously wounded. (*National Archives*)

The roof of the massive Car Shed lies in ruins after Sherman's men brought it down. The Concert Hall is in the background on the right. Photographer George N. Barnard made an astonishing visual documentary of the war in the West with an emphasis on Sherman in Atlanta, from September to November 1864. Unfortunately, much of Barnard's work was destroyed in the fire that spread through the city after Sherman blew up the remaining railroad, military, and industrial targets. (*Library of Congress*)

The Atlanta roundhouse is visible beyond the Italianate railroad station. (*Library of Congress*)

The Atlanta roundhouse was photographed from the tower of the railroad station before both were reduced to rubble. (*Author's Collection*)

Only a few masonry walls remain of the roundhouse. The facilities were shared by the Atlanta & West Point Railroad and the Georgia Railroad. The *O. A. Bull* stands prominently on the turntable. Other locomotives include the *Hercules*, the *E. Y. Hill*, and the *E. L. Ellsworth*. The locomotives without headlamps were yard workers used for switching and servicing nearby industries. (*Library of Congress*)

Union soldiers relax on boxcars at Atlanta. The flat cars are carrying fire engines. (*Library of Congress*)

Sherman's men are twisting Western & Atlantic rail in the Atlanta yard with levers that will bend it into useless spirals. To the right is part of the destroyed Car Shed. (*Library of Congress*)

A USMRR train chuffs by the ruins of the Atlanta Lard Oil Factory. America was still a country dependent on whale and lard oil for light and lubrication. It would be another 20 years before crude oil would be utilized to power the country. (*Library of Congress*)

Cars have been burned down to their trucks along an Atlanta siding. (*Author's Collection*)

The Battle of Allatoona was fought October 5, 1864. Confederate Gen. John Bell Hood sent brigades from his Army of Tennessee to destroy Western & Atlantic track, being then used to supply Sherman. The supply base at Fort Star was along the western side of the railroad at a deep cut in the Allatoona Mountain range. (*National Archives*)

This elevated guard post, overlooking the Etowah River, allowed soldiers to keep an eye on the important Western & Atlantic bridge (right). The Confederates, after destroying track in the district, intended to destroy the bridge as well. Allatoona Pass is in the distance. The battle there on October 5, 1864, was short but deadly with 1,600 combined casualties. (*National Archives*)

This deadly rail-borne battery was used at Petersburg, Virginia. The sloped faceplate was heavily timbered to resist gunfire from nearby snipers. Some rail-borne guns had faceplates sheathed with iron. After being positioned, the locomotive backed off to avoid being struck by the recoil of the car after its discharge. (*Library of Congress*)

The *Dictator* was a seacoast mortar capable of firing a 200-pound shell two miles. It did tremendous damage to Petersburg, Virginia. A special siding was built off the mainline, curving atop a ravine along the Appomattox River. The weapon could be aimed at various locations in the city by moving it along the curved track. The power of its first discharge shattered the car to which it was mounted. A sturdier one reinforced with iron braces was quickly constructed. The recoil sometimes sent the car 12 feet down the track. (*Library of Congress*)

A portion of Petersburg rail facilities lay in ruins. It is not known if this was the work of the *Dictator* or from the ceaseless shelling of the city from other artillery points. (*Library of Congress*)

The gun crew stands on the platform of the *Dictator* after it was decided to permanently emplace it near Battery #4. As much a weapon of psychological terror, it was effective in nullifying Confederate batteries on Chesterfield Heights. (*Library of Congress*)

When Union forces entered fallen Richmond the first week of April, photographers documented the unbelievable destruction. A locomotive sits shattered and scorched within the ruins of destroyed Richmond & Petersburg depot. The civilian at the front of the locomotive is the photographer standing motionless as an assistant counts off the seconds for the exposure. (*Library of Congress*)

Another view of the same locomotive, this time alone in the desolation of the R&P depot ruins. (*Library of Congress*)

The Richmond & Danville Railroad bridge was an ambitious combination of masonry spans and covered bridges. During the siege it took a heavy beating. (*Library of Congress*)

Piles of solid shot, canister, and other ammunition fill the yard of the destroyed Richmond arsenal. The Richmond & Petersburg bridge has track dangling off it. (*Library of Congress*)

An old style locomotive at the Richmond & Petersburg depot has been charred in the fireball from the near-by arsenal explosion. Its wood cab has been vaporized, leaving only its iron supports. Adjustable drive rods allowed for requartering the large driving wheels. Requartering—realigning the wheels with the axles—was a common adjustment to mid-nineteenth-century locomotives, particularly in yard engines that were constantly being jerked back and forth while making up trains. (*Library of Congress*)

A photo by Alexander Gardner shows the effect of Union artillery on the R&P bridge across the James River. (*Library of Congress*)

The destroyed area of Richmond was designated the "Burned District." In this view, lightweight rail dangles from a loading trestle right of center. (*National Archives*)

A bird's-eye view, top, shows the magnitude of the destruction in Richmond. In the foreground are the walls of the state arsenal. Delving into this view of the city reveals scenes of more railroad damage. Above, an old Pioneer-style locomotive sits charred and useless on a siding. (*Library of Congress*)

A look through the windows shows yet another destroyed locomotive.

Richmond women, dressed in black as if in mourning, walk amidst the rubble of their beleaguered city. (*Library of Congress*)

Former slaves and two white children they are in charge of pose on an island in the James River with the ruins of the R&P bridge in the background. (*Library of Congress*)

The Belle Island portion of the Richmond & Danville Railroad bridge was a combination of covered bridges and masonry. Union artillery destroyed the tracks between this covered span and the one to the far left. (*Library of Congress*)

Trucks are all that remain of rolling stock beside the Richmond & Petersburg depot. The passenger platform can be seen beyond the burned out station. (*Library of Congress*)

An iron bridge spans the canal near the destroyed Richmond & Danville depot. Sitting in the road are valuable locomotive tires probably salvaged by Union troops from the railroad shops. (*National Archives*)

Freed slaves, having gathered their belongings on a barge, travel along the Burned District on the James River and Kanawha Canal. They had greeted Lincoln upon his arrival at the city April 4, 1865, as a conquering hero. (*Library of Congress*)

A locomotive lies wrecked after the Richmond & Petersburg bridge it was sitting on was burned in the vicinity of Petersburg. (*Author's Collection*)

Charleston, South Carolina's, North Eastern Railroad station was blown up by Sherman's troops as were most other railroad related structures in the city. Railroad men, knowing Sherman was approaching, managed to get some engines and cars out safely over the North Eastern Railroad and the Cheraw & Darlington Railroad. (*Library of Congress*)

Columbia, South Carolina, suffered from devastating fires. Sherman said withdrawing Confederates started them. (*Library of Congress*)

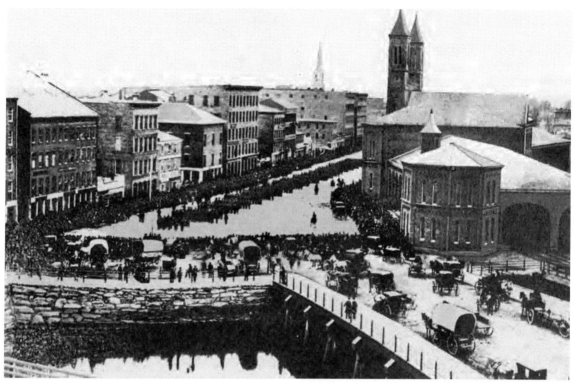

In stark contrast to the devastation of southern cities, Providence, Rhode Island, projects a sense of order. Citizens are welcoming troops near the railroad station. (*Author's Collection*)

The spectacular 2,500-foot long High Bridge over the Appomattox River near Farmville, Virginia, played a part in bringing an end to the war. It carried the much fought over South Side Railroad. A wagon bridge was carried underneath the tracks. The Battle of High Bridge fought April 6–7, 1865, involved attempts by the Confederates to burn the bridge. Union forces extinguished the fires and charged across the wagon bridge in pursuit of Lee. (*Library of Congress*)

A glimmer of hope remained with Lee's starving and ragged army when supply trains began arriving April 8, 1865, at Appomattox Station on the South Side Railroad. Hopes were dashed, however, when Union cavalry swooped down and drove the Confederates off. With his supply line cut, Lee signed terms of surrender the next day, Sunday, April 9. Remaining Confederate armies would soon follow suit. (*Library of Congress*)

Lincoln's private car stands outside the Alexandria shops after its completion. Built by the Car Department of the United States Military Rail Roads, it was christened the *United States*. Skilled craftsmen made sure it was the most richly appointed car in America. The *W. H. Whiton* has the honor of posing with the car. Lincoln was scheduled to give the car a test run the day he died. (*Library of Congress*)

SIX

BOUND FOR SPRINGFIELD
THE LINCOLN SPECIAL

"A lonesome train on a lonesome track—
Seven coaches painted black—
A slow train, a quiet train
Carrying Lincoln home again;
Washington, Baltimore,
Pittsburgh, Philadelphia,
Coming into New York town,
You could hear that whistle for miles around
Crying, Freedom! Freedom!"
—*Millard Lampell, The Lonesome Train*

The news came by telegraph and rapidly spread through cities and towns. Post riders hollered while riding by, "Lincoln's dead! Been shot!" The same day headlines stood across front pages in disturbingly large type. Lincoln was hated by many across the country. Critics feared him and some newspapers cruelly mocked him in insulting commentaries and caricatures. The event was a disaster nonetheless—another unbelievable challenge for a nation fresh from a brutal civil war. A hush descended on the country. Resentment of the man vanished, giving way to an overwhelming emptiness. A need to mourn as a nation—at least up North—rode in on the peal of church bells and the chuffing of the funeral train. With the rapid mustering that usually preceded a battle, prepa-

rations were made for the country's first national funeral. And again, the railroad would be called upon to use its war weary rails.

Newspapers richly detailed the event with a sudden abiding sympathy for the Lincoln family. Those that previously printed cruel depictions of Mary's unstableness mellowed into sympathetic references to her "frail sensitivity." This final disaster left her "fed up" with Washington City—as it was called then. Her wishes that her husband's remains be transported to Springfield quickly with no ceremony were twice over-ruled. She was badgered into submitting to a national spectacle. Mary was so devastated she could not even attend the funeral in Washington. She remained in the White House through the whole affair—a place that seemed to immediately reject her. The Lincoln's son William (Willie) was disinterred so he could be buried in the same cemetery in Springfield as his father. Willie died at the White House on February 20, 1862, of typhoid.

Mary simply could not bring herself to make the train ride. Dark thoughts of the corpses decomposing and giving off odors, even with the profusion of flowers, tormented her. She had been assured the injector (embalmer) who prepared Willie had done as good a job with the President.

Bolts of black crepe were unraveled. Buntings of red, white, and blue fret with stars were gathered at the corners and fastened to engine handrails and along the coaches of the funeral train. Volunteer bands prepared their instruments. Regiments were called again to march. Prized local hearses would bear the casket to places for public viewing. Bonfires were lit along railroad tracks so citizens waiting in the springtime night chill could catch a glimpse of the passing train, its coaches dimly illuminated in a solemn glow. Well trained in rapid dispatching during the war, the railroads involved quickly organized scheduling for the Lincoln Special—the official name of the funeral train. The War Department laid out the route and placed the railroads involved under military control. Brigadier Daniel McCallum, Director of the USMRR, would oversee the entire operation. The 1,654-mile route was, except for a few changes, the same route the president-elect traveled in his 1861 inaugural trip from Springfield.

The coach that would carry the remains had been originally built as Lincoln's private car. He was to give it a test ride the day he died. Named *United States*, it was designed and constructed at the USMRR shops at the Orange & Alexandria Railroad in Alexandria. Skilled carpenters and artisans had ornamented it with rich woods, brass and silver fittings, etched glass, enameling, and upholstered walls, making it the most luxuriantly appointed car in the country. It had a parlor and four lounge areas two of which could be opened into a long sleeping compartment for the tall President.

The original design called for two trucks but weight concerns led to four. The weight was now distributed more evenly over 16 wheels giving stability and providing a smoother ride. The truck pedestal guides were cast with fanciful details. The wheel and axle systems were adjustable, allowing the car to traverse standard or five-foot gauges.

Eyewitness accounts refer to the beautiful deep chocolate color paint and the luster it held from being hand polished with oil and rotten stone. It seems unlikely the coach would have been painted and then rubbed with abrasives that would have scratched and dulled the paint. If indeed it was rubbed, it was probably to polish varnish applied to the exterior mahogany superstructure. A bold colorful painting of the crest of the United States was located midway along the car in the oval ledger board. Other accounts remark on the exquisite hand-painted scrollwork adorning the exterior. This scrollwork was also applied to the large round-ended monitor along the roof.

The Lincoln Special chugged out of Washington, DC's Baltimore & Ohio Railroad Station at 8:00 A.M. Friday, April 21, 1865, under the mournful gaze of at least 10,000 citizens. The funeral train consisted of nine cars. This included Lincoln's private car (now his funeral car), a baggage car, and seven passenger cars to transport officials. The funeral car was draped in black crepe. The coffin of Willie Lincoln was in the car along with his father's.

A Guard of Honor remained on watch in the funeral car. The Lincoln's young son Robert rode the train 38 miles to Baltimore but then returned to Washington to be with his suffering mother.

Arriving at Baltimore at 10:00 A.M., the coffin was transferred by pallbearers to a hearse and then taken to the Merchant's Exchange Building, there to be opened for public viewing. An estimated 10,000 people passed the coffin in three hours. The train left the Howard Street station at 3:00 P.M. and steamed towards Harrisburg, Pennsylvania, arriving at 8:00 P.M. The coffin, again transferred by hearse, was taken to the Pennsylvania state capital and placed in a catafalque. Public viewing began at 9:30 P.M.

The hearse returned the casket to the funeral train the next day, April 22, at 10:00 A.M. after traveling down streets lined with 40,000 people. Pennsylvania engine #331, handled by Conductor George Phillips and Engineer J. E. Miller eased the train out of the city on the Pennsylvania Railroad. The train was run slowly, between 10 and 20 miles per hour to allow the throngs along the tracks a lingering look. It was something they would never forget. A pilot train consisting of an engine and coach preceded the Lincoln Special by ten minutes to make sure all was clear up the line.

At 4:30 P.M. after a trip of 106 miles, the train arrived at Philadelphia's Broad Street station. The structure, packed with mourn-

The President died April 15, 1865. Mrs. Lincoln did not want an elaborate funeral, desiring to get her husband's remains to Springfield, Illinois as soon as possible. She eventually gave in to demands for a national funeral—America's first. This is the last known photograph of Abraham Lincoln in life. (*Library of Congress*)

ers, was decorated in black crepe, patriotic bunting, flags, and spring blossoms. The hearse proceeded through streets lined with mourners. Arriving at Independence Hall, the casket was placed in the East Wing where the Declaration of Independence had been signed. The evening's viewing was by invitation only.

Along the way, people were allowed in the funeral car to view the open coffin. Newspaper reporters were given preference. Some wrote how his face retained the painful conflicts of his life.

The following day lines began forming for public viewing at 5:00 A.M. The public proceeded in two lines over three miles long from the Delaware River to the Schuylkill River. The wait was up to five hours; officials estimated the crowd at over 300,000.

The train left Philadelphia's Kensington Street Station at 4:00 A.M. Monday, April 24, and proceeded on the Philadelphia & Trenton Railroad to Trenton, New Jersey, where it transferred over to the Camden & Amboy Railroad. It continued on through Dean's Pond and Princeton. At New Brunswick a switchman stood diligently beside the switch throw he opened earlier to guide the pilot train onto the tracks of the New Jersey Railroad & Transportation Company. As soon as the Lincoln Special rolled through, he closed the switch.

Running evenly through Metuchen, Rahway, Elizabeth, and Newark, the special reached Jersey City at 10:00 A.M. and slowly entered the cavernous passenger shed. The clock inside the main terminal waiting room was deliberately locked at 7:20, the official recorded time of Lincoln's death. One report says the coffin was removed from the funeral car and taken by ferry across the Hudson to New York City; another says the entire car was ferried across.

A funeral cortege arrived at City Hall. The coffin was placed in a black velvet dais and at 1:00 P.M. the doors were opened to the public. As many as 500,000 people waited to pass the dais and pay their respects.

On Tuesday, April 25, Lincoln's coffin was placed on a magnificent 14-foot long funeral carriage drawn by 16 horses wearing long blankets. A procession of 75,000 followed the carriage through the packed streets. People paid up to $100 to rent a window along the route just to watch the cortege pass. A future president would catch a glimpse as the procession neared Union Square. Watching from his grandfather's second story window was 6 1/2-year-old Theodore Roosevelt.

The locomotive *Union* rolled out of the Hudson River Railroad station at 30th Street precisely at 4:15 P.M. taking the train through Manhattanville, Yonkers, Dobbs Ferry, Irvington, Tarrytown, Peekskill, and Garrison's Landing opposite West Point. It continued along the Hudson, passing Fishkill, New Hamburg, Poughkeepsie, Hyde Park and so forth, stopping briefly at some points to take on fuel and water. The train rolled into East Albany at 11:00 P.M. The coffin was ferried across the Hudson River to Albany and taken to the State House. Citizens were allowed to pass the coffin throughout the night. During that time the rest of the train was run up to Troy where it crossed the bridge spanning the Hudson and then headed back to Albany.

The next morning, April 26, a regal hearse pulled by six white horses bore the coffin back to the station. The streets were mobbed with onlookers. The New York Central took over the funeral train for the long 298-mile trip to Buffalo. There were brief stops at Schenectady, Canajoharie, St. Johnsville, Little Falls, Herkimer, Utica, Rome, Oneida, Syracuse, Rochester, and others. Families in small towns made long buggy rides to the more populated places where the Lincoln Special was scheduled to either stop or pass through. Railroad men stayed at crossings to keep the tracks clear as crowds gathered. Groups sang hymns, kneeled and prayed, while the retorts of cannon and guns reverberated across the hills. As the day wore on, the mellow hues of the April twilight appeared.

The first glimpse of billowing exhaust from the pilot train set hearts racing. Anticipation grew as the train blew its horn and sounded its bell while swooshing through a crossing. The funeral train was usually only ten minutes behind. If any music bands were present, they would start playing.

A murmur would move through the crowd as down the line people gasped, "Here it comes!" The tears would start rolling. Men removed their hats and held them to their hearts. People who had seen a hundred trains pass down these tracks would never again experience the sensations they now felt. It was as if the area were suddenly imbued with a divine presence. The tracks were somehow suddenly broader; the decorated engine appeared large, mighty, and of another world. The impressive cars, their wheels clickety-clacking over the rails, seemed larger than anything that had ever come through before.

As the train rolled into the darkness, waiting crowds lit bonfires to keep warm. Again noisy commotion announced its approach. Church bells chimed, guns and cannon were fired, music played. The funeral car was particularly haunting at night. The interior was illuminated, the light playing off the coach's white painted ceiling panels. The coffin was raised on a stand so it could be seen through the windows. Standing rigidly at each end was a member of the Guard of Honor.

People waited at stations late into the night. Waiting rooms were decorated with flags, black drapery, flowers, wreaths, and garlands of pine boughs. All of it took on a moody glow from additional candles and lamps.

Thursday, April 27, would be a stressful day. The train pulled into Buffalo at 7:00 A.M. A hearse drawn by six white horses draped in black took the coffin to St. James

Hall where it was view by 100,000 people including ex-President Millard Fillmore and future President Grover Cleveland. The nation was suddenly gripped by more stirring news. Lincoln's assassin, John Wilkes Booth, had been killed.

Conspiracy theories about what was behind Lincoln's murder were already being voiced. Even Lincoln's successor, Andrew Johnson, would be suspected of having a hand in the assassination. Johnson had been using the Washington Hotel as his residence. When Booth stopped in seven hours before the shooting, he left a card for the Vice President containing the message, "Don't wish to disturb you. Are you at home? J. Wilkes Booth." Of course this suggests Johnson was somehow involved but it is more likely Booth wanted to know his whereabouts. Johnson was supposed to be murdered as well as part of the larger plot. Secretary of State William H. Seward was brutally assaulted by one of Booth's conspirators that horrible night, but survived.

Nonetheless, Mary Lincoln firmly believed Johnson was involved in the assassination. She would later write her friend, Sally Orne:

> That miserable inebriate Johnson, had the cognizance of my husband's death—Why was that card of Booth's found in his box, some acquaintance certainly existed—I have been deeply impressed, with the harrowing thought that he had an understanding with the conspirators & they knew their man...As sure, as you and I live, Johnson, had some hand, in all this.

Others in the government suspected him but the Assassination Committee never uncovered anything suspicious. This was one of many intrigues surrounding the assassination that have kept researchers busy for generations.

The Lincoln Special would, during its April 27 run, travel down the Buffalo & State Line Railroad, then the Erie & North East Railroad. Later that day it would be directed on to the Cleveland, Painesville & Ashtabula Railroad which would bring it into Cleveland's Euclid Street Station around 7:00 A.M. the following day.

In Cleveland there was the usual ceremony and public viewing. The train later departed using the Cleveland, Columbus & Cincinnati Railroad tracks. Some of the railroad's engines saw service during the war. The Lincoln Special was pulled by #15, the *Nashville*. The locomotive was built in 1852 by the Cuyahoga Steam Furnace Company of Cleveland. The engine was certainly decked-out for the occasion. Its Russian iron boiler jacket had been buffed to a high gloss, as were all its brass and copper appointments. A picture of Lincoln was fastened to the pilot beam. Flags and crepe fluttered as the engine proudly brought the Lincoln Special to Columbus, Ohio on Saturday, April 29.

Eight pallbearers from the Veteran Guard would carry the coffin from the hearse to the rotunda in the state capital building. After a full day's viewing, it was returned to the funeral car and the train departed at 8:00 P.M. bound for Indianapolis, some 187 miles away.

From Indianapolis it continued to follow its rigid timetable, making stops, veering on to other railroads, until it arrived in Springfield at 9:00 A.M. on May 3. In all, the Lincoln Special traveled fluidly and flawlessly through 180 cities and towns in seven states and was viewed by an estimated 30 million citizens—nearly 65 percent of the population.

As it traveled down remote lonely tree-lined roadbeds, its wake stirred spring leaves as if dispelling the thousand questions Lincoln would have answered as to how America should move on. The train was about life's confusion over death. But as its whistle diminished far down the line, so would the impact of this last great event of the Civil War. The questions of how to move on would eventually be answered—rightly or wrongly.

The symbolic power of the funeral was profound. It helped elevate Lincoln as one of the greatest Americans.

As a railroad man unraveled the last strand of crepe from the last engine to pull the Lincoln Special, thoughts were already turning to getting trains back on their normal schedules. The embers in the engine firebox were extinguished so it could rest. Its sweat dried, as would the last tears of the whole affair.

When it was fired-up again for service, its throttle would be eased into welcomed peacetime commerce. The country was restless to move on. It needed desperately to move on. In the manner of trains that come and go, so would this terrible war in the long line of challenges America confronts in its pursuit of glorious, sustaining liberty.

The *United States*, carrying the remains of Lincoln and son William (Willie), stands guarded, awaiting its journey from Washington to Springfield. The route would essentially retrace Lincoln's 1,654-mile inaugural train ride in 1861. (*National Archives*)

The Lincoln Special left Washington's Baltimore & Ohio station at 8:00 A.M., April 21, with an estimated 10,000 citizens watching. The locomotive pulled nine cars; the funeral car, a baggage car, and seven coaches carrying high-ranking officials and their families. The train is pictured at Philadelphia's Broad Street station. The engine and cars were draped with black crepe. (*Author's Collection*)

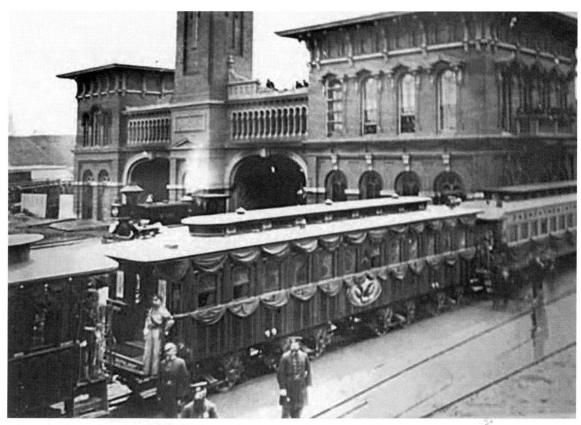

Along the route the car was opened for public viewing of the casket although it was mostly members of the press and dignitaries who were allowed on. Guards stand at the open doors of the car during its stop at Harrisburg, Pennsylvania. (*Author's Collection*)

Another view of the train at Harrisburg shows it with Pennsylvania Railroad's Engine #331. Along the route, a Guard of Honor stood at the ends of the opened coffin. A pilot engine and car was sent ahead of each run to make sure the track was clear. Thousands lined the tracks and at crossings to glimpse the Lincoln Special. They warmed themselves beside bonfires during the chilly springtime nights. Volunteer bands played music and at the first sight of the train, cannon and guns would fire. Church bells tolled. Stations were decorated with flags and crepe. The sight of the funeral car passing at night, illuminated with the Guard of Color at the ends of the open casket was profound. (*Author's Collection*)

Engine #331 is shown while uncoupled for refueling and service. (*Author's Collection*)

The *United States* is coupled with a Philadelphia, Wilmington & Baltimore car of similar design. The president's car, because of added weight, rode on four trucks. Along the route, the coffin was removed and borne by hearse to locations for public viewing. (*Author's Collection*)

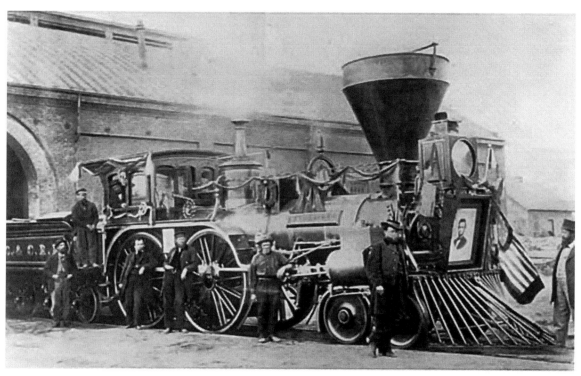

The *Nashville* of the Cleveland, Columbus & Cincinnati Railroad was assigned to take the train from Cleveland to Columbus on April 29. Railroad officials pose with it outside the Cleveland engine house. Note the portrait of the president attached to the front of the engine. The train left Cleveland's Euclid station at midnight and arrived in Columbus at 7:00 A.M. The president's coffin lay in state in the rotunda of the Ohio State Capital until evening. (*Library of Congress*)

This view of the *Nashville* was taken at Cleveland's Euclid Street Station. Eight railroads would be involved in the tightly scheduled run. The Lincoln Special would pass through 180 cities and towns in seven states and be viewed by thirty million people—nearly 65 percent of the population. (*Library of Congress*)

Scenes such as this in Columbus, Ohio, were typical in major cities where pallbearers brought the coffin to a hearse. Processions would accompany the hearse as it made its way down prominent streets to locations for public viewing. (*Author's Collection*)

The train is visible beyond this elaborate pagoda over the hearse on Chicago's 12th Street. (*Library of Congress*)

Contrasting with the president's spectacular funeral is this view taken in April 1865 at a hastily dug cemetery near Richmond. These would have been future doctors, teachers, inventors—loving husbands and fathers. A soldier mourns at a friend's grave. At least these fallen soldiers had wood markers, crooked as they are. (*National Archives*)

The Lincoln Special, standing on Chicago's waterfront pier, is ready to depart. It would travel over the Chicago Alton & St. Louis Railroad to Springfield, arriving at 9:00 A.M. on May 3. The next day President Lincoln's and Willie's remains were conveyed to Springfield's Oak Ridge Cemetery. (*Author's Collection*)

Among Lincoln's greatest legislative achievements were the Pacific Railroad Acts of 1862 and 1864, authorizing the building of the First Transcontinental Railroad. The ceremony for driving the golden spike at Promontory Summit, May 10, 1869, officially opened the railroad connecting the Atlantic with the Pacific. It was tremendous technological achievement that helped smooth the troubled waters left by the war. The Great Emancipator would have been proud. He was, after all, a railroad man at heart. (*National Archives*)

BIBLIOGRAPHY

BOOKS

American Locomotive Engineering by G. Weissenborn. Glenwood Publishers.

The Charleston & Hamburg by Thomas Fetters. The History Press.

Civil War Railroads by George B. Abdill. Bonanza Books.

Civil War Railroads & Models by Edwin P. Alexander. The Fairfax Press,

Grant Takes Command by Bruce Catton. Little Brown.

The Growth and Development of the Pennsylvania Railroad Company by H. W. Schotter. Allen, Lane and Scott.

A History of the American Locomotive: Its Development: 1830-1880 by John H. White, Jr., Dover Books.

The Life of General William T. Sherman by James P Boyd. Publishers' Union.

The Northern Railroads in the Civil War 1861-1865 by Thomas Weber. Indiana University Press.

Plantation Life on the Mississippi by W.E. Clement. Pelican Publishing Company.

Plantation Parade by Harnett T. Kane. William Morrow and Company.

The Pennsylvania Railroad: A Pictorial History by Edwin P. Alexander. Bonanza Books.

The Railroads of the Confederacy by Robert C. Black III. University of North Carolina Press.

Southern Storm: Sherman's March to the Sea by Noah Andre Trudeau. Harper Perennial.

Stealing the General: The Great Locomotive Chase and the First Medal of Honor by Russell S. Bonds. Westholme Publishing.

This Republic of Suffering by Drew Gilpin Faust. Vintage Books.

INTERNET RESOURCES

Academic Medicine (journals.lwww.com/academicmedicine): "Ambulance Trains," February 2001, Volume 76, Issue 2.

Aeragon (aeragon.com), First Modern War.

American Civil War (americancivilwar.com), Battle of Fort Donelson.

Appalachian Blacksmith Association (appaltree.net/aba/index.htm).

Battles for Chattanooga Museum (battlesforchattanooga.com).

Charleston & Hamburg Railroad (railga.com/charlhmbrg.htlm).

Civil War Preservation Trust (civilwar.org).

CSA Railroads (csa-railroads.com).

CWSAC Battle Summaries (nps.gov/hps/abpp/battles/tvii.htm).

Harpers Ferry National Historical Park (nps.gov/hafe).

Historical Marker Database (hmdb.org).

History of Wetplate "Collodion" Photography (alternativephotography.com).

Library of Congress Online Catalog (loc.gov/pictures).

Library of Congress, Railroad Maps, 1828–1900 (memory.loc.gov/ammem/gmdhtml/rrhtml/rrhome.html).

Lillian Goldman Law Library (law.yale.edu/library).

National Railroad Historical Society (nrhs.com).

NC&StL Railway Preservation Society (ncstl.com).

New Georgia Encyclopedia (georgiaencyclopedia.org).

North Georgian History (ngeorgia.com/history).

Petersburg National Battlefield (nps.gov/pete).

Picture History (picturehistory.com).

Railway Preservation News (rypn.org).

Telegraph History of the Civil War (unitedstatesmilitarytelegraph.org).

U.S. National Archives Photostream (flickr.com/photos/usnationalarchives).

INDEX